# The Badge and the Brain

### Street Smart Force

# by Dr. J. Franklin Shults

Copyright © Joel Shults  2012

The Badge and the Brain: Street Smart Force

# Table of Contents

**Introduction**

**Why Should I Read This Book?**

**Basic Braining**

**Survival First**

**Close Encounters of the F3 Kind**

**Let's Get Physical**

**It Takes Two**

**What Rats Know**

**The Broken Brain**

**How Your Smile Can Kill You**

**Let's Talk about You**

**Afterword**

# Introduction

Much is spoken of my father's era of Americans, described as the "Greatest Generation." These were men and women who arose from a stifling depression, won a cataclysmic world war across the planet against two gigantic evil empires, then worked to create the greatest era of science, education, and industry in history.

I am one of the children of this great generation. As part of the baby boom, I was a child of the sixties and a young man of the seventies. I was sworn in as a civilian police officer in 1978 and joined what I believe was a great generation of police officers, serving at the dawn of massive technological and social change. Officers of this era saw the arrival of communication technologies that radically changed policing. The active courts during the civil rights era changed the rules of engagement for state and local cops. No occupation was more immersed in opening its ranks to women and minorities than law enforcement. Law enforcement rapidly evolved, embracing education and training initiatives, meeting the challenges of civil unrest, facing rising crime related to drugs and gangs, and eventually even combating terrorism.

I hope to be one of many practitioners, leaders, trainers, and researchers now leading the way into yet another fascinating frontier of science, one that will provide policing with fresh approaches to serving the public. This frontier is literally within us: it is the human brain. As I have read book after book and study after study, I have been astounded to find things that I've learned over my thirty-five years in the law enforcement business confirmed by recent brain science. I would often exclaim or sigh aloud while reading as I realized how much this research could help police officers do their jobs.

I began my reading looking for insights into stress-related disorders, as I saw a need for increased mental-health awareness both for my fellow officers and for myself. I then had to become an expert in human capacity and decision making while dealing with a shooting within my department. Then, on an even more personal note, my brother was nearly shot by a deputy after she gave him a death notification. My brother had gone into a grief rage, and the deputy did not know the difference between anger and aggression. I don't fault the officer for her lack of training, but I knew from experience that that kind of reaction was within the range of normal, and not deadly-force aggression. I began to read more about the brain's response under threat to see if my own experience had a scientific foundation. Indeed, it does.

As a result, I decided to put forth this book. It is not a scientific treatise, but rather a simple narrative of my recommendations based on my reading in the context of my real-world experience. The material I have used is open source and not proprietary; therefore, unless I reference a specific quote in the text, I will dispense with extensive notation. I will, however, provide a reading list at the end of the book.

Given the vast and fast-changing body of knowledge about the brain, I have kept this work fairly short and simple. This is not because I think police officers cannot handle academic works, but because I know they are busy and want to hear what works and why so that they can put the knowledge to use. I hope that what I share makes your career safer and more successful, and your life less stressful.

# The Badge and The Brain

## Street Smart Force

## Chapter One

**Why Should I Read This Book?**

The information in this book will make you an even better cop than you already are. Think of warriors throughout the ages. What do you see them doing in between battles while gathered around a fire? They were probably sharpening their swords, repairing worn gear, oiling up a critical piece of equipment, or cleaning their weapons. Whether you think you have a lot to learn about the business (and I hope you think that, no matter how good you already are) or you have already achieved superstar status, there's always opportunity to sharpen your sword. That's what this book can do for you.

One of the things I've learned about a lot of cops is that they love learning new stuff, but they are skeptical of anyone who claims to have new information. You may be thinking, "So what? Am I really going to do anything differently if I know how my brain has been working behind the scenes all my life? I'm doing fine as it is!"

My answer to you is YES—*you WILL change*! This brain stuff is foundational to almost every aspect of excellent policing. Let me put it this way: if you knew of a physical exercise that would give you a big advantage over the next resisting arrestee, would you at least consider reading more about it? If there were a little trick or two that would increase the number of confessions that you got from suspects, would you be interested to hear it? The information I'm offering will build on and affirm much of what you already know, so it's not so much "new" information, but information that will validate and enhance many of the things you already know and use.

The application of brain science can lead to improvements in many aspects of police work:

- better treatment of officers involved in use-of-force events

- reduced use of force

- better ability to articulate "suspicious" behavior

- higher rates of confessions and admissions

- more effective training and retention

- better supervision and management of personnel

- earlier recognition of physical and mental health issues affecting productivity and morale

- more insightful investigations and greater understanding of motive and crime scene behavior

- *a calmer, more professional demeanor*

The great thing about a lot of what you will read in the coming pages is that you already know a lot of this stuff—you just didn't know you knew it! Every person and every officer has characteristics and skills that may be sharper than other colleagues' and maybe some areas that could use improvement or that we don't use or care about that much. For example, I am pretty good at dealing with emotional people, probably because of being somewhat of the family mediator when I was growing up. Other cops would often ask me to deal with unruly juveniles, death notifications, and suicidal persons. If any of them had asked me to teach them crisis intervention techniques, I wouldn't have known what to tell them. It was just natural for me. But after doing brain research (and a lot of intervention training over the years), I now know the biological reasons why some of the things I do actually work.

So, what are your strengths? Are you a good fighter? Do you have a great sense of when someone is lying to you, or when someone is about to run or attack? Are you good at teaching? Supervising? Calming people down? What do your colleagues ask for your help with? Whatever it is that you're good at, if it involves human behavior—including your own—then **this book can make you better at it**.

What frustrates you about your law enforcement career? Is it your relationships at home? Your crazy schedule? Are you getting too many use of force complaints? Do you get so nervous during qualifications that your performance suffers? Do you wish you could get more confessions? Again, if your challenge involves human behavior, this book will help.

Now, you might be saying to yourself, "The brain is about thinking and feeling. I don't care about that psychological stuff—I just want to be the best cop ever." That's exactly why I wrote this book. The brain is ultimately about actions. All the thoughts and feelings in the world are meaningless to us unless we act on them. Do I care how a drunk is feeling? Only if it affects her behavior and how I can most effectively get her into custody without a complaint.

*The Badge and the Brain* is about getting your job done more effectively with less hassle. Do you want more civilian complaints that are going to interfere with your promotions and assignments? Do you want a lawsuit hanging over your head month after month? I don't! If reading this book could reduce the possibility of any of those career-limiting occurrences by even 10 percent, wouldn't it be worth it? I think so.

And just one more thing that I know my readers are worried about: that I'm going to advocate being Officer Nice, avoiding conflict at all costs, claiming that you can deal with everybody, no matter how crazy they are, without laying hands on them, and getting a thank-you card after every arrest you make. That's not my program.

From an officer safety perspective, knowing more about the brain is more likely *to keep you alive*. You'll be better able to discern a real threat from an ego threat, identify truly dangerous behavior, and not only take down an aggressor faster and earlier in the contact, but also be able to better articulate why you acted as you did before any prosecutor or jury.

***If you need to hit somebody, take them down, or even kill them, this book isn't going to talk you out of it.*** The information in this book will help you make a more informed decision about when those actions may or may not be necessary.

As civilian police officers, we have the same problem that our soldiers have had in Iraq (and Afghanistan and Vietnam): determining who the enemy is. In a war where the good guys and bad guys aren't wearing different uniforms, the decision to use force depends on the soldier's determination of whether or not a person in a combat zone is a combatant or an innocent civilian. But "collateral damage" is more forgivable in combat than in civilian policing.

The Badge and the Brain: Street Smart Force

In our world, we must minimize any suffering of the innocent. Even if we have probable cause to take someone into custody, that doesn't automatically make that person a combatant. Everyone we deal with is a threat risk, but that threat varies widely from person to person, moment to moment, and situation to situation.

Let me tell you a couple of stories. One involves my brother Phil. When his two sons were in their late teens and early twenties, one of them—my nephew Craig—was shot and killed after an argument. Craig's killer was later acquitted. You don't have to imagine how draining that loss and the subsequent trial was on the whole family.

Only about a year and a half later, Craig's surviving brother, Scott, was settling in to trade school in another state and seemed to be getting along well. Those of you who have been struck by deep grief can understand that no one in the family had "gotten over it," as is often expected by others who have moved on. Scott had been a real strength to his family during all of the difficulty. As often happens, however, Scott never revealed—and perhaps didn't even recognize himself—how crushed he had been. Shortly after Scott had moved into a new apartment, his roommate found him dead from a self-inflicted gunshot.

Now we fast-forward to the rookie deputy who got the call to give notification to Phil and his family that Scott was dead. She drove alone to Phil's country home and knocked on the door. After going inside, she delivered the terrible news. Grief and shock affect people in different ways. With Phil, on this occasion, the reaction was rage. Walking away from the deputy and into another area of the room, he stomped and stormed in circles, then picked up a potted plant and threw it against the wall. The deputy, alarmed, drew her service weapon and brought it up while my sister-in-law yelled at her not to shoot. Everyone did calm down, and a double tragedy that was seconds from becoming a monumental calamity was averted.

That is the story that made me write this book.

I know that because my brother was involved, my objectivity is tainted. I also am hesitant to second-guess a police officer's decision since I wasn't inside her head or even in the same part of the country when the event happened. But as a veteran officer and former law enforcement chaplain, I realize that my brother's actions were quite normal. I also know that the type of anger he displayed was not aggression against the officer (although that certainly can happen). How do I know? Even in his deep rage of grief, he directed his aggression away from the officer.

Many of us, based on our years of personal experience with people under the influence of high emotion, would have intuitively felt less threatened than our young deputy colleague. Even so, few could have explained exactly why. There are observable physiological characteristics and behaviors that can help officers interpret anger and aggression, but while many of us are trained and experienced in reading those signs, *few of us are trained in how to describe them.*

I've seen misinterpretations in the field. Many times an officer will fail to recognize signs of danger that should be met with immediate response. In other instances, like that of the deputy in my brother's case, the misinterpretation results in an officer's unnecessary escalation of tension. I believe that the failure to recognize signs of danger is more common than the misinterpretation of those danger signs.

I was privileged to put brain knowledge to work to defend an officer who was criminally charged with a felony assault after shooting a burglary suspect. The investigating officer from a state agency combined a set of erroneous and disappointing assumptions in the warrant request. The document revealed a serious lack of understanding about the brain and how we perceive danger and react under stress.

I was able to examine the report and point out the reasonableness of the officer's actions. The officer was actually acting quite heroically and appropriately under the circumstances. It was a profound error for him to have been criminally charged. Fortunately, there was a favorable disposition in the case, so the officer escaped with no criminal record, but *his career was effectively*

***destroyed by an investigator who was ignorant of how the brain works.***

Maybe at this point you're excited and can't wait to learn more about how brain science can improve your life and work. If so, let's get started! If not, maybe I should address one more possible objection that some readers might have against this book: me, the guy who wrote it.

Cops can be skeptical and hesitant to accept instruction from someone they have no reason to trust. (There are brain science reasons for this too, by the way!) Some people look at my background and see that I hold a doctorate in education rather than psychology, that I've been a university professor, and that I've been a police chief. I've also never worked in a large urban law enforcement agency, or a state or federal agency. Some cops don't want to hear from somebody they perceive as over-educated, or who hasn't served on the mean streets of whatever they think is worthy. Some think that an administrator loses all memory of how the real world operates. If you're one of those folks, give the book a read, and if what you find doesn't seem to work for you, pass it along to somebody else who might be interested.

I'm choosing to keep this book as simple as possible because I know that my readers are busy and can find out more technical information on their own. You can go online and get lots of maps of the brain with all of the areas and medical names. The truth is you'll be able to remember more concepts if you have less extraneous information to process, so don't be offended if you think I'm going overboard on dumbing things down.

For our purposes here, we are not concerned with matters philosophical or metaphysical. We will only talk about how our body responds as a result of what goes on in the brain, not how the brain knows we exist or how we have a sense of self.

I also won't be footnoting or referencing within the text, but you'll find a helpful reading list at the end of the book.

Now, let's get down to the basics!

## Chapter Two

**Basic Braining**

The brain has three essential functional areas that I will reference throughout this work. I call them ***the lizard brain, the linking brain, and the logic brain***. A quick Internet search will yield a number of brain diagrams that will point to regions and components of the brain, along with their proper medical nomenclature. If you decide to do more research and reading on your own—which I highly recommend—you'll recognize what I'm talking about. For now we just need to know how these three functional parts affect how we behave.

The ***lizard brain*** manages the simplest life functions. It does essentially the same thing in humans that it does in any other creature: it keeps your heartbeat and breath going, and it makes you run away when you're threatened. It's the part that's connected to the base of your brain.

The lizard brain has only one concern: keeping your body alive. It is very sensitive in interpreting threats to your well-being and will react instantly, without "thinking." The lizard brain operates largely in stealth mode. Although it does not have ultimate control over our long term behavior (we do have free will choices that we make using all of our brain areas), it does have authority to bypass other parts of the brain and make a decision that can ***direct our body functions and***

***behavior without us realizing what's happening***. Your lizard brain—called that because it is so primitive and simple in its purpose—commands a number of the body's chemical producers.

Part of what the lizard brain does is adjust body chemistry. These chemical changes are often described as emotional responses. We talk about fear, anxiety, nervousness, panic, suspicion—"gut" feelings—but they are ***not really mere emotions***; they are interpretations of chemical changes and neurological activity initiated by the lizard brain.

In addition to influencing our feelings, this body chemistry change affects body function and behavior. We attribute our quick reflexes to our training and our identification of something "suspicious" to our intuition, but these are functions of our lizard brain calling out before we are consciously aware of it, based on experiences as far back as infancy.

The ***logic brain*** is behind the forehead and does the job of thinking rationally. The logic brain is charged with making good decisions based on all available facts. It is the part of the brain that we think (wrongly) governs most of our conscious behavior. The logic brain is the executive decision maker. Theoretically, your logic brain is a master calculator, a measurer of risk and benefit tapping every resource of memory and information stored in the whole brain to make a behavioral decision. That behavioral decision may be to make a purchase, engage in a relationship, speak, or sit down. One of the most interesting aspects of our ability to make logical decisions is that, for the most part, we don't. And we shouldn't. Decisions made without emotion are not always best.

In between the lizard and logic brains lies the ***linking brain***. Here is the storage area for all of the information used by the logic brain to make those flawlessly rational decisions. Memories, including the memories of emotion, lie here like books in a library, ready to be checked out as needed.

You can think of these three areas as a runaway stallion (the lizard brain) tugging on a chain (the linking brain) being held by you (the logic brain) trying to maintain control.

The general location of these three functional areas is of great interest to scientists. For our purposes, I just want us to remember the idea of messages being sent from the lizard brain up through the linking brain to the logic brain. Take your index finger and place it on the back of your neck at shoulder level, then trace a line up and across the top of your head to your forehead. If you don't want to do that you can just visualize it (which you already did anyway, right?).

This motion is a good way to remind yourself to move from lizard thinking to logic thinking. Say the word "think," and draw out the vowel ("thiiiiiink") while making the lizard to logic motion. If you don't want to say it out loud right now, you can vocalize it in your head (which you also already did, right?). This little reminder will be of enormous help in remembering to calm yourself in a tense situation, or to visualize your goal when trying to calm others. We want to go from lizard to logic (uh-huh, visualize the motion and the word "think") when we have time in order to take ourselves off of autopilot and regain control.

Of course, you've noticed that I'm employing brain science to help readers remember these foundational concepts. I've kept the number of items to three very manageable elements: lizard, linking, and logic. I've also used the memory device of alliteration—each of the mind's functional areas starts with the letter L: Lizard, Linking, Logic. I've encouraged you to do a body motion (tracing from lizard to linking to logic) to engage you physically. You have also visualized that motion, along with thinking and saying "thiiiiiink." You have been exposed to the words "lizard," "linking," and "logic" several times in order to take advantage of the memory power of repetition. And finally, you were given a mental picture of a powerful horse pulling a chain that you're holding as an illustration of the sequence, tension, and interaction of the three functional areas.

As we read or hear information, we have a memory process that decides what will become a permanent part of our library for later decision making.

We can't hold on to everything or there would be just too much information to manage. Therefore, information that comes to our attention must prove its value to us pretty quickly or it gets pushed out. If the information has some usefulness, it sticks.

That's why I'm using methods that will help get this foundational information filed in a significant place in your linking brain library. This also models some methods you might want to use when you have something you need to remember. If you are a trainer for your department, you can remember some of these to use when you're trying to help students remember important items. (And if you are a trainer, you've already filed and retained this information because you recognize that it has significance to you).

It is the *linking brain* that does a good job of moderating both the screams of the lizard brain for survival and the calm, rational reflection of the logic brain. The linking brain reminds the logic brain of the emotional cost of decisions, and is most closely associated with how we feel in terms of our mood and outlook on life. Each memory that we have is stored in a variety of sections of our brain. When we see something, we not only have a visual image that is stored, but *an emotional and environmental context that becomes part of that memory*.

For example, my five-year-old granddaughter, Madelynn, was visiting and wanted to go to a favorite secondhand store where we would often go to buy her an inexpensive book or toy. Between visits the manager had moved the toy section forward and had replaced the display in the back corner of the store with small appliances instead of toys. Madelynn rushed past the new location (with the toys prominently displayed) and instead stood, perplexed, looking at the small appliances and wanting to see toys.

My daughter, fascinated by the developmental stages of her child, wondered aloud why Madelynn was still asking where the toys were and insisting she was in the right place even when it was clear that the toys had been moved. Madelynn's visual memory of the toy section was quickly contradicted by her current view, as well as the view of the toys now in their new place. Her emotional memory, however, was still in the corner display area. While her logic brain was saying "The toys aren't here," her linking brain was accessing emotional memories that said "Here's where Grampa brings me to get toys."

One of the misconceptions about the brain is that it is rigidly divided into areas of function. We do know that the response to particular stimuli is linked to certain general regions of the brain. During some types of brain scanning, the brain is described as "lighting up" in certain areas—for instance, when the subject is listening to jazz, viewing erotic images, or making a decision in an experiment. We know that the brain is constructed of two sides held together with connective tissue, and that the left brain dominates some characteristics of human behavior and the right brain others. We also know that when certain areas of the brain are affected by injury or disease, memory, perception, mood, and personality can all be altered.

We also now know that ***the brain can change***. It can even use a part of itself for a new purpose. For example, if a person goes blind, the area of the brain that previously had been used for interpreting visual images can sometimes repurpose itself for other uses.

It is a false formula to say that we are "x percent nature" or "y percent nurture"—in other words, that there is so much about us that is biologically predetermined that there is little we can do about it, and that the rest of our personality and behavior is so deeply ingrained by society and our environment that there is little hope for change in that regard either.

The idea that we are "left-brained" or "right-brained," in terms of determining personality, has much basis in fact but is still a vast oversimplification of how things work. The old saying that we only use a small percentage of our brain is also misleading. A normal brain has as much capacity as needed for whatever our body wants to accomplish, short of violating the rules of physics.

What we do know for sure is that the brain is a network that accesses multiple regions and systems during decision making, that it has an amazing restorative and "plastic" ***ability to remake itself***, and that we can intentionally leverage our knowledge of how the brain works to effect change in our lives. We have the power!

The brain is like a jetliner on autopilot. Most of what our body does is so rehearsed, based on experiences as far back as infancy, that we aren't really aware of it. Like the jetliner's pilot, if we become aware of something that we need to take control of, we can override the autopilot. We might get all kinds of warning signals, but we can still struggle for the controls and steer the aircraft.

Like a path beaten down by cattle from the field to the trough, our frequent activities happen "mindlessly"—an ironic term, since our brain already works at a constant level of sub-awareness. Do you take the same route to work every day? If you do, you know that you don't have to think about how to get to work from your driveway. You don't need to get out a map and plot the route. You don't need to look for landmarks to let you know you're almost there. You don't even need to watch for stop signs and speed limit warnings. Your brain already has all that information programmed into your hands on the steering wheel and your feet on the pedals.

You probably don't even have to look at the speedometer to know that you're going at your normal speed. The visual cues from passing landmarks allow your brain to calculate that. The pressure of your foot on the gas pedal and your fingers on the steering wheel are well practiced. You might even get to work and not even remember the trip!

But what happens if the street department decides to put in a new stop sign, or if some driver runs through an existing one? How do you feel if you've had a crash a few months ago at one of the intersections you pass on the way?

Your trip might feel different if you are driving a car that you don't usually use. The well-worn paths in your brain that guide your trip won't work quite as well. New paths can be created pretty quickly as the brain supplies memories of other driving experiences to help you learn the new and slightly different variations of the new vehicle. You might turn on the windshield wipers trying to hit the turn signal; your brain will perceive that something is wrong and correct your behavior so that you won't do the wrong thing very often before you learn the ergonomics of the unfamiliar turn signal location.

As a side note, it's interesting how minor a change can be to affect your movement. For example, I usually wear a snug, low-profile holster since I'm more often in plain clothes. When I wear my uniform, with my equipment belt and duty holster, my gear increases the width of my waist and I spend the day banging into office furniture and door frames. The extra inch or two of width changes my navigation! For trainers, these minor equipment variations can be very significant and give testimony to what is commonly called "muscle memory," which really is just some well-worn paths in the brain, as it is the brain that tells the muscles what to do. It would be best if all of my holsters had the same release systems, since having even a slightly different feel or position takes a toll on my ability to get my firearm out under stress.

Now let's use the variations to your commute that I mentioned previously. As you pass by the intersection where you had a crash a month ago, you always get a little extra cautious. The intersection is no more dangerous now than it was at the time of the crash, but the memory of this particular leg of the trip has an emotion chiseled into it. That emotion changes your behavior. Your perceptions are enhanced. If you are very self-aware, you might find that your grip tightens and your foot hovers a little closer to the brake pedal. You might even find that your pulse rate has increased slightly and that your muscles are tighter. This is a result of your linking brain attaching the emotional experience to your decision making process.

Remember: understanding the brain ultimately means understanding behavior. Emotion affects behavior. ***Emotion is processed as memory*** and is found in the linking brain.

On your first commute after the crash, you might have felt an urge to take a different route. Decisions can be processed on several different levels: at a very high awareness level in the logic brain, just beneath awareness in the linking brain, or automatically in the lizard brain. The urge to take a different route may be influenced by all of those brain function areas. If you begin consciously thinking about the decision or desire to change routes, your logic brain may take over the process. The logic brain will consider factual information, perceptions, and emotional context and probably decide that it doesn't really make sense to alter your commuting route.

I'll talk about PTSD and related brain health issues in a later chapter, but a person doesn't have to have a traumatized brain to be influenced by past experiences. Whether we are aware of it or not, our decisions and behaviors are all a collection of past experiences. *We are calibrated to avoid things that may harm us and to seek things that make us feel good.* So not only will you naturally want to avoid an intersection where you experienced a threatening event, you'll also probably have at least some degree of reaction to any similar intersections or anything that might remind you of that crash.

Speaking of threatening events, this is where the lizard brain excels. The lizard brain, in cooperation with the other brain functions, has only one goal, and that is to keep your body alive. It is the lizard brain that ignites the chemical process that enables the body to behave in one of three ways when danger is present. The body will react by preparing to *fight for survival, flee from a threat, or freeze and shut down* to create a smaller target or preserve essential core body function.

Let's say on today's commute you're on autopilot when a car blows through a stop sign and screams into the intersection just as you start to enter it. Your lizard brain gets visual and auditory data signaling that something is a threat: a couple of tons of high-velocity metal are on course to crash into your space. Although primitive, your lizard brain knows that if you took the time to process your decision through your logic brain, there's no way you could respond in time to avoid the crash.

The lizard brain has been endowed by nature with the power to take control, at least temporarily, of the brain's decision-making process. To do this, the lizard brain releases a deluge of chemicals—including adrenaline, which enables the body to perform in unusual, sometimes superhuman ways—to respond to the perceived emergency. *These biochemical messages sent by the lizard brain are so intense, they can burn a path into the memory that can affect nearly every perception and decision* made by all of the brain's functional areas.

In this book, for simplicity I'll refer to that chemical stress cocktail simply as "adrenaline," though in fact there are a number of different chemicals and brain connections at work in what we refer to as an "adrenaline rush."

## Chapter Three

**Survival First**

*The brain's sole function is to manage behavior in a way that best ensures survival.* This central truth informs your ability to make sense of the brain science applications that lead to being a better cop. This truth also will come in handy later, when I introduce some techniques for dealing with other people which may seem counterintuitive.

You already know, I'm sure, about the fight-or-flight response. What I want to emphasize in this book is how pervasive that brain function is in human behavior. It is not something that happens only with dramatic events. It is a daily, constant, driving force. A large part of how you as an armed government agent can be at the top of your game is by applying this principle in your work in a consistent way. Don't save the knowledge for a special occasion. You can make use of it the very next time you're on duty!

Survival first is still a great and necessary part of our brain's function. But the reality is that most people don't live in a world full of the same kind of threats that people encountered prior to our current, more civilized society. I don't mean that we are any better behaved or have a greater moral code than at other times in history (although I could argue that we do), but rather that we are a highly regulated society that is designed to stifle some of the very instincts that the brain equips us with.

I'll mention here that ***the other function of the brain, secondary to survival, is the pursuit of pleasure***. Sensory experiences, whether they be sight, sound, touch, taste, or smell, can drive us to seek to repeat a pleasant experience (a survival-enhancing experience) or to avoid an unpleasant experience (one of no use to survival or reproduction). Some of what we think of as purely mental experiences, such as being "high" on drugs, are also sensory experiences, even if the sensations are internal to the mind.

If our brain function could be reduced to a simple binary system, it would dictate that we actively avoid pain and actively seek out pleasure. Yet ***most of our moral code is devoted to regulating pleasure seeking***.

Police work is, in its essence, a battle against the most basic human drives. You as a law officer are a part of the control mechanism that keeps society from chaos and anarchy. Most people can self-regulate, delay gratification, and empathize with other humans who also suffer in our shared pursuit of pleasure and avoidance of pain. But those who do not self-regulate, we must socially regulate. For those who do not respond to social norms, we have created a coercive agency to force that conformity. That is us—the armed agents of the government. ***It is our role as brain and behavior***

***regulators that brings us into direct conflict with others.***

Believe it or not, twenty-first century America is about the safest, least-violent place ever known to the human race. The modern world, with a few vicious exceptions, presents fewer violent threats to human life now than at any time in human history.

Now, when I say that we are relatively safe in our modern nation, I am not including you! As a police officer, you get invited to all kinds of conflict and danger. You get called to situations that in times past would have to have been handled by victims, their families, or some vigilante group.

Luckily, even in the modern world, our instinct for self-protection, preprogrammed into the brain's wiring and chemistry, is still working. When the lizard brain perceives a threat, it responds by attempting to override the logic brain in order to take defensive measures immediately.

What would be considered a threat? Certainly an attack by a human or other vicious animal, or a disaster like an avalanche or flood, constitutes a threat to survival. The body will be commanded to actively resist, run, or play dead. This is commonly referred to as the ***fight, flight, freeze (F3) response.***

Since we have few of those kinds of life-threatening events in our lives, it might seem that the F3 system would lie dormant. However, the lizard brain considers lots of things to be threats. Threats to our ego, our sense of identity, our property, and our general control over our lives all count as threats and all generate the F3 response.

Now that you know that the F3 response is constant and primary, and that the brain's processes manifest as behavior, you can put this knowledge to good use.

One of the things that surprise me about myself is that I forget that my job exists to deal with dysfunction. I remind both my officers and myself that almost everyone we meet is under the influence of F3. Complaining that it seems like everybody we encounter is a nutcase is like a doctor complaining that everyone she sees is sick!

Your very presence will ignite F3 in most people, even in a positive interaction, at least to some degree. Keep in mind that F3 lies on a continuum; some reactions will be severe, some very subtle. Let's review what F3 looks like.

The lizard brain does not care about the future. It only cares about making sure you survive for the next few minutes. In fact, at full effect, the body can only survive the F3 dump of chemicals and resulting behavior for a short time. Shock or exhaustion can lead to cardiac arrest in extreme conditions.

On the subtle side, F3 can change blood chemistry, pulse, and respiration and can affect sensory perception and muscles at levels that only medical instruments can detect.

F3 is often identified as stress. Stress is a biological response to a perceived threat and is often expressed as an emotion or sensation. People may say, "I'm so nervous," "I'm stressed out!" "I feel like throwing up," or "I'm freaked!" F3 stress is the result of a set of chemicals being pushed through the body to prepare for action and injury. Normal body activities such as digestion, libido, and immune response are robbed of resources when the lizard brain runs roughshod over the rest of the brain.

To anticipate injury and quicken healing, the composition of your blood changes to improve coagulation and provide more glucose for energy. Blood is diverted away from its normal distribution to supply the major muscle groups that might be needed for gross movement. Your pupils will dilate to see better. You may jettison unnecessary weight in the form of urine and feces. Senses of taste, touch, smell, hearing, and sight become more intense as well as more selective.

From your experience and training, you know that these physiological changes occur in nervous people. The shaking, cold hands are a result of circulatory changes, as is the flushed or pale skin, dry mouth, nervous energy, and stomach upset.

These signs of stress are important data for your decision making when dealing with people. It may be to your advantage to increase their stress or, in most cases, to reduce it. Knowledge of F3 effects is also critical to your own health and demeanor, as we will discover in another chapter.

To illustrate F3, let us use the model of a rocket on the launch pad. (Image courtesy of NASA)

F3 requires an ignition source. That ignition is whatever the brain interprets as a threat. Recognize that F3 launches based on perceptions of danger, regardless of whether the danger is real or not. I was a bit of a scaredy-cat as a child. At night, after the lights were out, some clothes on the back of a chair would morph into a seething monster ready to pounce on me. My fear reaction was real, even though my monster was not.

Some people with a low threshold for fear and stress (including those with PTSD and related anxiety disorders) are always primed for a quick F3 response. Officer survival experts often talk about this readiness in terms of being at condition yellow, red, or black. They advocate that police officers should never relax except in an environment that is completely free of threats.

But a place completely free of threats may not exist for cops. Memories of threatening events, worries about future problems, conflicts at home over finances, relationships, and crazy schedules all can cause the F3 to heat up and bring us closer to "launch."

***The logic brain is the only brake that can slow or stop the lizard brain*** from pushing ahead with the F3 response.

The perception of danger by the lizard brain is the fuse that ignites the chemical cocktail of F3. I've only watched NASA launches on television. The huge space shuttles seem to need a push to get off of the ground, then slowly burn their way into the sky. Military rockets with explosives shoot out of their mounts like bottle rockets. Movies use countdowns and last-minute aborted missions, burning fuses, and ticking clocks to create tension in viewers.

Any time a police officer comes in contact with another person, the conditions exist to light that person's fuse and launch the F3 sequence. ***Every contact, then, is an exercise in aborting the F3 launch.***

# Chapter Four

## Close Encounters of the F3 Kind

Let's get to the most important benefit of brain science in law enforcement—dealing with dangerous people more safely.

One of my days that I survived just by the grace of God, I was driving on patrol as a rookie and saw a young couple arguing. It looked like things were going to get physical. I called out on a pedestrian contact instead of a possible domestic, so no one was in a hurry to back me up. I expected to tell the couple to calm down and move along.

When I stepped up to them, I did so without any tactical consideration of maintaining distance. I was in counselor mode and had none of the advantages of nature's fear chemistry.

Then I saw the knife in the young man's hand. It was a pocket knife with the blade extended. The knife was the subject of the couple's animated conversation. He said he was going to stab himself, and she was against that plan.

So now I was up close and personal with a suicidal person holding a knife, with the naïve and innocent girlfriend tugging at his arm. I managed to grab his clenched fist and lock his arm long enough to convince him to let go of the weapon. There was nothing good about the quality of that encounter.

What was it about the young man's demeanor that made me feel safe enough to approach him, then safe enough to spend time talking him into relinquishing his weapon?

First, let me get past your thinking about this scenario. I know you're replaying it in your head! This was daytime, by the way. I should have called out my contact more accurately, advising dispatch that I was out on a male and female arguing, and given a clothing description. From behind cover, or at least from a tactically sound distance (out of knife-lunging range), I should have given a command or request for one of the pair to come to my position and talk to me.

I had potential peace disturbance charges, so I didn't have to worry about this being merely a consensual contact from which they could lawfully walk away. From a position of advantage to me, I could have made additional observations about the demeanor of both of them, including posture and body language that may have revealed that he was holding something, even if I couldn't tell what it was.

After either seeing the knife or seeing him concealing something, I could have taken an appropriate response posture, given verbal commands, and called for backup. The rest of the conversation could have happened after he was safely handcuffed and searched.

Of course, anything could have happened had I responded that way. He could have taken off running, she could have shielded him, he could have taken her hostage—the variables are infinite. But I wouldn't have been inches away from the point of a knife!

Remember, I promised I wouldn't try to convince you that there are foolproof ways of dealing with people that will always work to gain compliance. We are given tools and rules about force for a reason: sometimes people have to be forced to comply.

Many readers have taken communication courses or read the late Dr. George Thompson's book *Verbal Judo* or had some other method presented to them. These measures all have value, and all have the potential to be used appropriately or misused. There does not exist one ultimate solution to all communication issues, including me or this book.

Now, back to the question of what made me feel so foolishly comfortable ambling up to this guy.

From the time we are out of the womb, we begin studying faces. Scientists have learned that this process is amazingly complex and very necessary. The interaction between the mother and infant is a mutual teaching and learning process essential to survival.

Through this interaction and others, as a baby's social world expands, humans learn the ***meanings of facial expressions, verbal inflections, and other body language*** such as proximity and touch. The depth of this understanding is the foundation for ongoing learning. It happens to all of us (absent some brain glitch or malfunction) and continues throughout our lives.

By the time you became an adult, you had a mental catalog of thousands of individual faces and thousands of variations and combinations of nonverbal communication cues. Most of these patterns are not at the awareness level. These images are heavily laden with emotional and contextual cues from all of the senses that were at work while building the memory. I was walking through a mall far from home years ago and started looking around for my Aunt Maxine when I smelled her perfume, even though it was quickly clear to me that someone else could be wearing that same scent!

Not long ago, I met a new family at my church. My wife and I were invited over to their house for a meal. We had a great visit and fun conversation, but I couldn't understand why I had a bad feeling about the husband. I engaged my logic brain to examine this problem and eventually realized that he had a smile that was just like a former colleague of mine—a colleague who was egotistical, backstabbing, and opportunistic. My linking brain was alerting me subtly that this guy might be egotistical, backstabbing, and opportunistic. Once I brought that to my awareness level, I was able to get that intrusive thought out of the way and enjoy the company of our new friend.

We process these images automatically, without having them analyzed by our logic brain, unless (perhaps after reading this book) we ***practice bringing our brain functions to high-awareness level***.

I am avoiding using the words "conscious," "unconscious," and "subconscious" because I am not a psychologist and may not use them in the medically correct way. Also, these words may have slightly different meanings to other laypersons. What we are really talking about, whether I use the Freudian language or not, are ***levels of awareness***.

Keeping it simple, awareness may be at a very high level—for example, the sun is up in August in Missouri, and I'm aware that I'm hot!—or it may be at a subtle level. It rains overnight as I am camping in September in Missouri, so I stay bundled up while making breakfast. As the sun rises higher, I become less comfortable and realize that I am now too hot to be wearing that wool sweater, so I make a logical decision to take the sweater off to be cooler. I likely was feeling the effects of the increasing temperature before my discomfort reached a high level of awareness. In other words, even before I became highly aware, my body was likely already trying to adjust my skin temperature by working with my sweat glands, respiration, and body movement to cool things down.

Often our awareness is an internal awareness. Our body knows something that our brain hasn't told us yet. By the time we get to the point at which we can assign language to our awareness, it already has reached a high level. So, we have been feeling warm for some time before we say "Gosh it's hot in this sweater!"

As I've said, most of our inner body and thought behavior occurs at a level of non-awareness—rehearsed, automatic, and on autopilot. It is a professional skill and advantage to be able to turn some of that subtle internal awareness into high external awareness. That's what this book is all about.

Much of our interpretation of the intent, meaning, relationship, and so forth of behavioral cues—including speech patterns—occurs on autopilot. My family often enjoyed the sometimes wicked game of people watching on busy sidewalks and making up stories about the lives of complete strangers. The remarkable thing was that we always tended to agree on the storyline based on what we were seeing. We all had similar responses to the facial expressions and body language of our unwitting subjects. I suspect that if we had stopped and interviewed some of them, we would have been very accurate in our guesses about their life stories unfolding at that moment in time!

It is a good exercise to sit in a coffee shop, mall, restaurant, or hotel lobby and deduce the nature of relationships. Are they married? First date? Business meeting? Siblings? You likely would come up with some accurate conclusions, but trying to articulate all of the reasons why you came to those conclusions would be challenging.

The reason we might be unable to explain why we draw a particular conclusion about another person is that the cues are often a collection of very tiny clues. We've all heard body language experts talk about the meanings of certain movements and postures. Facial expressions can last just milliseconds. Vocal inflections can be slight. You can probably tell a sincere smile from a well-intended fake one all because of a very slight difference in the way the skin appears. Even our sense of smell can be at work at the non-awareness level, telling us that someone is nervous or attracted to us.

So back to knife-boy. At the time I had the encounter with this couple, I was a rookie and had not yet experienced the full range of behaviors and emotions, nor their physical manifestations. (In the years since then, I've seen it all!) Therefore, I hadn't yet compiled the large file of behavioral cues that my brain now holds. I interpreted the young man's behavior as merely annoyed and somewhat agitated and angry. I put out of my mind the idea that this might be a lethal encounter. The scenario didn't fit my template for being on full alert.

Nothing in the young man's behavior screamed suicide drama. Looking back, I now understand that the reason I didn't get that "vibe" from him was that his behavior wasn't coming from the lizard or linking brain—it was coming from his logic brain. He was constructing an act for the sake of drama and manipulating his girlfriend. Although good acting can bring forth very realistic behavior, this drama king was faking it, and his body wasn't buying into it. Therefore his body language, gestures, and facial expressions were not congruent with a violently suicidal person.

My brain, then, at a sub-awareness level had already calculated from all of the sensory data that there were no genuine danger cues that I recognized. I should add that my recognition of danger cues was based at that time on my very limited experience as a police officer. I had not yet trained myself to look for a weapon on EVERY encounter, and I hadn't had enough brushes with death and injury for my brain to make an emotional and survival connection to the vast number of risk factors I now know.

Can I characterize this as a non-dangerous situation? No! The young man's brain could easily have switched from posturing for his girlfriend to posing a real threat after I entered the picture and called his bluff, and he felt his ego threatened. However, my perceptions were correct at the time, and even though I had no external awareness of why I had acted so casually, I survived because knife-boy's brain didn't have the heart to follow through on a threat that was never real in his own mind.

The encounter did add several new patterns to my mental playbook, however. The moment of adrenaline upon seeing the knife only after I had walked into a kill zone made that memory quite permanent. I survived and learned.

# Chapter Five

**Let's Get Physical**

***The body will reveal what the mind is processing, and it will do so with great precision to the informed observer.*** This is the key for every champion poker player and every gifted interrogator.

One of the things that really fascinated me as a young cop was what other cops saw that I didn't. My very first ride-along as a high school student was my introduction to the "sixth sense." The veteran cop I was with on a midnight shift seemed to have twenty sets of eyes as he spotlighted, car stopped, and checked out all kinds of things.

Many years later, I was the object of that same kind of fascinated curiosity. My wife and I were hosting some college students from our church, and it was time to get the pizza. One of the students went along to help me carry all of the pizzas we had ordered (and to protect the pizza from me). As we passed an intersection, I saw a woman walking near the corner and I said to myself aloud, "Wonder what's going on there?"

The student heard my muttering and looked around. Seeing what I saw, but without the benefit of experience, he asked what I meant. I told him something vague, like "I dunno, just didn't seem right," and we went into the pizzeria to pick up the order.

On the way back home, we passed the same intersection and saw that there were now two police cars at the scene and an ambulance with the woman. The young college student looked at me with a sense of awe and wonder: "How did you know?" To tell the truth, I wasn't sure how I had known that something was amiss.

Later that evening, I spent some time bringing that internal awareness to my logic brain in order to find the answer to the young man's question. I was already teaching patrol procedures at the academy and had discussed recognizing suspicious behavior. I realized that most of my illustrations were of such obvious stuff that they didn't take much work to recognize as suspicious. Even then, as a fairly experienced officer, I had not highly developed **the skill of bringing the internal awareness out of autopilot and activating the external awareness of the logic brain**.

If I had been on duty and needed to justify a non-consensual contact with the woman, I would have probably not been able to articulate all of the factors in a report. As I began listing the things that made me "alert" to the woman, I realized that this was an area of town with bars and restaurants, but only the bars were still open; that seeing a solitary woman was fairly unusual; that there was no other pedestrian traffic present; that the woman was not moving with purpose (she paced, then stopped, then turned, then walked back); that she was looking around as if lost or disoriented; that she was overdressed for the area in terms of style; and probably a few other micro-cues that I didn't ever register on an awareness level.

None of those cues individually would have meant much, but the constellation of behaviors sent out the larger message that something unusual was going on. I don't remember if I ever found out what all the fuss was about, however; I got too engrossed in my pepperoni.

The practical lessons here are twofold. One is that people will show in their behavior what is going on in their mind. The other is that we make informed assumptions about the meaning of others' behavior with sophisticated accuracy but at a non-awareness level in the brain.

The law officer who practices the skills of bringing autopilot thoughts to a high awareness level—labeling the behavior that they observe and the subsequent justifiable assumptions about the meaning of that behavior, and then articulating those observations and conclusions in a report—will have well above average success.

A primary sign of what we will simply call suspicious or guilty behavior is dissonance. By that I mean the indefinable discomfort you feel at seeing things that don't make sense. Another term is *incongruence—things not lining up the right way*. The reason they don't make sense is that they don't square up with the learned patterns of behavior we have in our brain's library of human behavior.

This little twist in your brain is the square peg trying to fit in a round hole. The peg is what you are observing or perceiving, and the hole is the template of your experience of what is normal.

You've seen the old familiar comedy script where the husband comes home and the wife is super sweet to him? We know these characters enough to know that this couple is always bickering, or he is henpecked, or she is always catching him doing something stupid. But tonight she's made his favorite meal, greets him with a big hug and kiss, and asks about his day. The comedic tension builds and the poor guy doesn't know how to respond to being treated so nicely!

Finally you see his eyes open wide with the realization that he's being manipulated. He likes being treated this way, but it's so unusual that he finally says something like, "Wait just a minute! How bad was the damage to the car?" We all laugh because we enjoy knowing ahead of time that the wife is acting out of character because she has bad news to tell him.

The husband had a preconception of what was normal. Within a preset range of behavior, the beaten-down paths in his brain had a few possible scripts for his arrival home; being treated with respect wasn't one of them! His wife's behavior, in context, just wasn't adding up.

The problem with dissonance is that it is uncomfortable, just like an out-of-tune piano. Unlike you, most folks haven't trained themselves to analyze the source of this discomfort and bring it to active awareness level in order to discover its significance. Instead, they create a thought process that makes the feeling go away.

My wife and I were walking on The Plaza in Kansas City, Missouri, a few years ago looking for a coffee shop. She's a veteran cop's wife and has some good instincts. She noticed a man walking alongside the driver's side of a line of cars parked on the street. As he walked along, fairly rapidly, he was glancing inside the vehicles he passed.

Think for a moment how a person would normally find his parked car. Imagine it. Many people would already have their keys out. They would know at least approximately where their car was, and their sightline would be directed toward that location. Looking for your car is a common and shared experience.

If the man were walking at a normal speed, he would make the usual social contacts with other people on the sidewalk. He would make quick eye contact, perhaps smile or even say hello, and then look ahead again. If he were to walk in the street, it would only be when he was close to his car and not for a long distance, and even then he might look at his watch or his keys as a signal to bystanders that he had a purpose.

So even though you probably haven't had to answer the question "How does a guy look while walking down the street to get into his parked car?" *you have a template in your brain of a collection of behaviors* that you would expect for that common situation, partly because you've probably had that experience yourself, and partly because the combination of social interactions, however slight, and physical movements associated with this scenario are easy to piece together from past experiences and observations.

What my wife saw was not what she would expect to see. The man was in the street instead of on the sidewalk. He was focused on the inside of the driver's side of every car he passed. When we try to find our car, we look at color, make, and license—big or familiar characteristics. We don't look inside a car to make sure it's ours unless there is a car just like ours. The man never looked up to acknowledge any other human being nearby, nor did he make the socially acceptable false movements we do when we want to avoid eye contact with others for some reason.

My wife nudged me and told me something wasn't right about that person. Like a good off-duty cop out of my jurisdiction, I followed him for a while to see what he was up to and eventually spooked him enough that he disappeared. I don't really know what he was up to, but I agree with my wife's theory that he was looking for something to steal.

Would most people be as adept at spotting suspicious behavior as a veteran cop's wife? If they were paying attention, they probably would feel a degree of discomfort, a sense that something wasn't right. But an unskilled observer probably wouldn't be able to put a finger on what it was that made things seem odd. Most people would deny that anything was wrong, tell themselves that it was none of their business anyway, have a moment of self-preservation and change direction to get away from the situation, or create a narrative for themselves that could explain away the situation.

The tension that comes from the square peg can be reduced by creating a story that rounds the peg off enough to make it fit in the hole. So, the casual observer might rationalize, "Hmm. He must be looking for a friend's car," or some other plausible explanation. Once there is something to make that person believe that the unusual behavior is actually normal, the mind settles a little and life goes on.

**The brain-trained police officer, however, senses the dissonance and allows it to be a signal.** He or she mentally draws a line from the back of the brain to the forehead, signaling that he is now going to turn off the autopilot and move from the lizard brain to the logic brain in order to uncover the factual, behavioral basis for the feeling that something is suspicious. He begins to thiiiiiink!

The sad thing is that some officers never develop this skill. They don't listen to that feeling. They miss the signals or make up a reason to ignore them. On a campus where I once worked, there were hundreds of 911 misdials because it was necessary to dial "9" to reach any off-campus number.

We had to answer all of those calls, since we couldn't know which were bogus and which might be real. We didn't run hot on those calls because the statistical probability was miniscule that the call was a distress call. I was once with a less experienced officer when a 911 hang-up call was dispatched. When the dispatcher gave the location of the call, I told the other officer to come with me and ran to the patrol vehicle to get to the location. I could tell that the other officer was surprised at how seriously I was taking the call, but didn't say anything since I was the boss.

When we arrived, we discovered a domestic violence incident in progress. Afterward, the officer said I had made a good call to run hot, but wondered why I had treated this one like the real deal. I explained that the vast majority of 911 hang ups came from elevators and administrative offices, but this one came from a family housing unit. In other words, it was a little out of the norm, so I paid attention to that little "hmm" in my head and responded accordingly.

I'll never forget the year our whole town's water supply was rendered unusable by an outbreak of salmonella. Potable water distribution points were set up throughout the community, and one of my civilian employees was assigned to protect one site. He had orders to stay out of the hot summer sun and to get appropriate relief from time to time, but he was too heroic to take care of himself.

Later that night he sent me a nonsense text. He asked part of a question about the next day's assignment, followed by gibberish. Something wasn't right. No college-age person would text that badly! I sent an officer to check on him—he was incoherent and suffering from heat exhaustion. The officer called an ambulance and got the worker hospitalized.

The officer was amazed that I had diagnosed a medical emergency long-distance just by a scrambled text. But I had learned to listen to the voice of dissonance like an alarm bell. Something didn't seem right, so instead of explaining away the weirdness by assuming that he was drunk or that some kid had gotten hold of his cell phone, I followed through with my suspicions.

***Accepting your autopilot, low-awareness, "gut" feelings as a signal to action is only the first stage on***

***the path to being a superstar law officer.*** Many great cops have a good handle on this. They let that dissonance sound an alarm to remind them to think that feeling through with their logic brain. The proper response to that alarm is to ask questions until you have a good, factual answer for what the suspicious behavior or circumstances might mean.

The second stage is accurately interpreting behaviors or circumstances. My account of my brother's anger and the deputy's misinterpretation of that anger as dangerous aggression is a perfect example of the importance of this step.

The third stage is articulating your thought processes and observations in a way that convinces a prosecutor, judge, and jury that you had every reason to make contact, handcuff, or even shoot.

# Chapter Six

**It Takes Two**

I'm sure that you have a good handle on the first stage: accepting your gut feelings as an alarm bell to think about what you're sensing. Please practice! Gain a new enthusiasm for studying human behavior. Find a public place and start observing (without being so obvious that you end up with a restraining order). Try to guess what people are talking about just by their body language. Interpret their emotional states and their relationships to the people they are conversing with. How is each party in the conversation reacting? Are they fascinated? Enlightened? Skeptical? Bored? Trying to be polite but totally turned off?

Now practice identifying, as specifically as you can, what is leading you to those conclusions. I find this fun and still do it! What you're doing is establishing a more finely tuned library of "normal" templates. This will make unusual, dissonant, or suspicious behavior show up in even greater contrast and detail.

Humans perform optimally with the right amount of stress. Too little and we fail to do the things we should. This is called "routine" or "complacency." Too much adrenaline and we tend to do things we shouldn't, because our body is saying DO SOMETHING, even if it's wrong.

If I could give you a homework assignment, I'd ask you to go to BLUtube, YouTube, and any other sites where you can find videos of persons attacking law enforcement officers. When you get a chance to do that, look for the behavioral cues in body language, movement, proximity, verbalization, and environmental context. Watch to see if the officers involved are paying attention and accurately interpreting the cues.

There are some very painful scenarios in these videos that are extremely relevant to us in this discussion. One type is where the offender's behavior is clearly dangerous and the officer continues to make verbal commands instead of using lethal force. The officer's senses are functioning normally, just as ours are as we watch and hear the video. What is not functioning at a rational logic brain level is the brain's interpretation of the event as one in which the officer must kill his or her assailant. (Yes, I know—"stop the threat" is the preferred language, but that's policy, not brain-based behavior. The brain-based behavior is to kill).

So what's going on inside the mind of an officer faced with a deadly assault who fails to use deadly force in return? Simply stated, there are a lot of badly constructed templates about what to do in a situation like this.

One possibility is that the officer has never definitively, explicitly, and intentionally had a frank discussion with him or herself about killing. We know that good and decent people are reluctant to kill, including soldiers in combat. An officer may take pride in talking himself out of danger. He may have had great success with that skill and may never have mentally rehearsed successfully engaging a human target with lethal force. At some level, all of his training has been compartmentalized away from the reality that he may have to kill, so that is the program that kicks into gear. He's rehearsed not shooting a human being, so that's how he behaves when the real situation presents itself.

A second possibility is that the officer has considered having to kill, but only in very clear and scripted situations. Believe it or not, we are trained by television and movie cops. The images we see, in which we become emotionally involved because we identify with those fictional characters, become a trampled path that our brain uses to make autopilot decisions. If an officer only imagines being confronted with a shotgun at a bank robbery, he or she may perform picture-perfect if ever confronted with an obvious bad guy wielding a shotgun at a bank robbery. But if that same officer is confronted with a 23-year-old woman with a knife in an apartment kitchen, the officer may not even consider deadly force because it doesn't fit the rehearsed pattern.

A third possibility is that an officer overestimates his ability to react to a threat. A sidearm may remain holstered. Cover and concealment may be abandoned. He has been trained to win every shooting in every training scenario. He has a positive, winning mindset. He waits until the threat presents itself very plainly, then finds that the eighth of a second he has to react and pull the trigger just isn't enough in a real-life encounter.

A fourth possibility is that the officer is overwhelmed with brain activity and suffers the "freeze" component of the F3 response. Unlike law enforcement officers, bad guys don't have to try to remember department policy, consider lawsuits, or deal with the moral code of deadly force as a last resort. There is no corner of their mind that makes them think the other guy is owed a verbal warning or the first shot. The bad guys don't think about how poorly they did on the last qualification day at the range. The bad guy doesn't concentrate on sights or center mass. He does not look downrange for innocent bystanders. He just shoots, because that's what he had intended to do if it came to that.

A fifth possibility is that the expected behavior of a shooter or attacker may not fit the library file of expressions, body language, and verbal and nonverbal cues that the officer has learned to associate with being attacked. There may be no evil grimace, no screaming, no fleeing. In scenario training, officers playing bad guys are always just acting and therefore cannot replicate the whole array of micro-behaviors associated with a real killer, nor are they able to show all of the vocal and physical signs of a genuinely violent attacker. While role playing is a very important training technique, it can never convey the total reality of lethal behavior.

What would you add to this list of reasons why a police officer might not use deadly force in a situation in which you think you would? Have you had a frank conversation with yourself, a trusted friend or spiritual advisor, or veteran police officer about your ability to take a human life?

An understanding of brain science can help us act more quickly and appropriately as we understand the behavior of aggressors and our own decision-making mechanisms. While underreacting can get us killed, overreacting can kill our career and destroy innocent lives.

Researchers have identified a variety of anxiety behaviors, defensive behaviors, and aggression behaviors, and what they have found is that not all lizard brain panic responses are equal. One interesting finding is that surrender can be a survival mechanism in the animal kingdom. "If the odds are that I'm going to die," the rat thinks to himself, "maybe if I submit I'll only be injured or the big cat will just go away." It may not be good for the rat's ego, but he may live to reproduce!

Posturing is also present in the animal kingdom. Hissing, growling, or other noisemaking can put an aggressor on notice that the animal is ready and able to fight. The aggressor may decide to find another, more passive target. If not, the noisemaker may decide to run or surrender to the superior force.

Territorial defense and family defense are also found in the animal kingdom. Everyone knows that a dog or bear will be much more aggressive around pups or cubs. Once they successfully remove you as a threat to their babies, their need for aggression recedes. (Of course, it's different if the bear is hungry. That kind of aggression is much more persistent!)

To end a territorial or family-defense-based aggression, you must remove the threat that they perceive. This may involve some level of disengagement or redeployment. For the police officer, making an adjustment like that will come as a threat to their own sense of control and identity, and their own F3 chemistry will ratchet up.

The real option lies outside the F3 chemistry of the lizard brain. Once again, draw that imaginary line from the back of the neck, over the top of the head to the forehead, and allow the logical brain to take over. If you have time to think, thiiiiiink!

Let's take a traffic stop. A man is driving with a woman and children in the car. You tell him that you observed him fail to signal a few blocks back. He starts to show signs of agitation, then says, "Oh, this is bullshit. Do you even know who I am?"

How are you going to respond? The first rule is *if you have time to think, then think!* That's the first rule of the logic brain. If a situation requires immediate intervention, then let your training kick in and do what you need to do. But if there is time to think—even a few seconds to breathe—then take that time to articulate the behavior of the violator and to become aware of your own behavior.

This may involve redeployment. Unless you need to engage in combat for your own safety—and again, I never take the force option out of the question—it sometimes makes sense to redeploy. **Redeployment is not the same as flight**, although it might look the same to an outsider. It is merely repositioning for a tactical advantage in order to win.

As a police officer I would never run or back down from a threat. However, if I need to tactically disengage and redeploy to get the job done, I will. "You mean run away?" the skeptic might ask. No. I simply leverage my options, tactically disengage out of the threat zone, and redeploy to best activate my available assets.

You may have to create distance, find cover, or just get out of a person's space to help the other person calm down. I once stepped into a person's personal space directly from the front because I was going to go toe-to-toe to prove that I was not intimidated. I was immediately knocked unconscious. The next time I found myself being driven by my ego instead of sound tactics and self-control, once again stepping into a violator's personal space, I decided I'd redeploy and stepped back to continue the conversation. That one ended better.

For some reason, as mild-mannered and easygoing as I am, I have this trigger point when someone challenges my authority. Mere noncompliance doesn't get to me—it has to be a certain attitude of disrespect. I've had to work hard, and still do, on recognizing the precursors to that trigger in order to keep my F3 in check and act professionally and appropriately.

What's your trigger? If you can recognize it early, draw that imaginary line from your lizard brain to your logic brain and put it at an awareness level. You then can take time to redeploy and think about how to best handle the encounter.

While never completely outside the influence of emotion, the logic brain can recognize the ego, status, and peer pressure elements of the F3 responses. Remember that physical threats aren't the only thing that sets the lizard brain in motion. ***Threats to identity, ego, territory, and life goals can be just as powerful***. The logic brain focuses on the rational goals: you want to resolve this situation safely and without generating a complaint or lawsuit.

First, let's become aware of your own mind and body. You may quickly label the violator an asshole or something similar. What the brain is doing is dehumanizing that violator to allow you to treat the person as less than human and therefore giving you greater permission to harm him.

You may flash back to previous offenders who acted this way and predict this violator will behave the same way. If the interaction with the previous offender who acted this way had a good outcome, you will mentally expect that pattern to repeat itself. Knowing that the outcome is likely going to be okay, your own perception of threat is lowered, in turn lowering your F3 response.

But if the previous interaction with a similarly behaving violator ended badly, your anxiety will increase. You may actually act in a provocative way to get to the conflict quicker and get it over with. This is the same mechanism sometimes seen in domestic violence. You arrive at the assault scene and the suspect tells you how badly the victim was behaving and that she should know that just makes him that much more angry. As you review the argument, you have the passing thought that you'd be pretty mad too if you were treated that way. One possible explanation for the behavior is that the victim knows from past experience that a beating is coming her way and thinks she might as well get it over with so that the terrible anxiety of waiting can be skipped. So she does or says something highly provocative and gets her punishment.

What is more miserable—the shot, or sitting in the waiting room knowing you're going to get a shot? It's the anticipation that creates the anxiety.

So, with this obnoxious violator, the lizard brain figures you can go ahead and drag him from the car and 'cuff him, since you know how this is going to end anyway!

But the logic brain scans the environment. You notice that the swearing violator doesn't make eye contact but looks down, ahead, or in the rearview mirror. He's not really focusing his anger toward you. That's a good sign. You assess that he's defending territory or family. You decide to ask him to step out of the car. That distances him from his defensible territory and removes that part of the threat that you present to him.

Add a little humanizing: "Sir, I know this is uncomfortable to everyone. A lot of people get upset when they are pulled over." That doesn't validate his opinion or agree with his argument, but it does accept his emotion, and that will help him get his thoughts from the lizard brain to the logic brain. And that's always good.

Once again, don't think that I'm bending over backward to accommodate a jerk. If at any time you need to get him on the ground in handcuffs, do it! I just want you to win using your superior knowledge and skills, and to accomplish your goal of taking enforcement action and making the roads safer. That never means relaxing or deciding that there is no threat.

Any kindness must be "tactical kindness," otherwise your brain will shift from "Watch this guy!" to "Aw, poor guy needs a break." Your brain chemistry, body language, and reaction time will all shift slightly to accommodate this attitude. A predator or psychopath will sense this and attempt to use it to gain a tactical advantage.

Your deep sense of awareness of your own linking brain's operations and the ***intentional shifting of your thoughts toward logic and strategy just helped you avoid acting emotionally***.

He'll get his ticket, you haven't invaded his family's nest, you haven't threatened his ego status with the children, and he didn't have to watch his wife's "I told you so" facial expressions. You simply helped him shift to his own logic brain to deal with the situation.

## Chapter Seven

**What Rats Know**

Much of the early research on stress was done with lab rats and other members of the animal kingdom. That's a good idea because animals don't necessarily behave better just because somebody is watching them. They also are less likely to sue if they get a probe implanted in their brain or take an electric shock when they want to get a food pellet.

In her book *The Biology of Violence*, Debra Neihoff states that a world devoid of aggression would be biologically unreasonable. In other words, there are good and natural reasons why we have the mechanisms of F3 chemistry. She goes on to say that anger is not the same as fear biologically; defensive and protective aggression manifest differently. Protective behavior is different from indiscriminate lashing out.

Neihoff notes that aggression that is impulsive and explosive is generally not criminal, purposeful, or premeditated. My brother's explosive reaction to hearing of his second son's death fits that category. If you've been around the block a few times on calls with angry people, you'll recognize the behavior. Wall-punching, hats thrown on the floor, tight circles of pacing, and self-hitting are all behaviors that the individual confines to a space that intentionally doesn't invade your space or get physically pointed in your direction. Depending on the circumstances, it is often best to let this person rant and rage if there is a somewhat controlled environment.

These bursts of activity will often burn off quickly. The supply of F3 chemicals for this kind of event is not indefinite. Time and activity will naturally slow this kind of individual, just like the fuel burning off during liftoff in our rocket analogy.

The person is often ready to listen to you fairly quickly. Because his rage is internal and not directed toward you, the officer on the scene, he is likely to comply if you make a general request for him not to leave or to drop that vase. If you can no longer tolerate his behavior or someone is at risk of getting hurt, move to an appropriate intervention. But the main point is that this person doesn't usually need to be shot, shocked, or tackled, because his aggression will resolve on its own.

An officer's ***aggressive response can trigger a shift in the subject's anger*** from being directed at Fate to being directed at the officer, changing the encounter into a self-fulfilling prophecy of personal violence.

You should test a person for their ability to be rational. How in touch with his or her own logic brain is the person? Persons deeply under the influence of F3 chemicals may be oblivious to your presence, unable to hear your voice, or helpless to tame their inner stallion in order to immediately comply with your commands. This is definitely not the time to ask questions that require much thought. "Tell me what happened" is an unreasonable request of someone who may be unable to think clearly.

Asking a person's name or a simple yes or no question like "Are you okay, man?" might get a response of "Fuck you" or "NO I AM NOT OKAY," but that tells you that he has the capacity to hear and understand you.

This is also a point at which you will naturally get some F3 messages from your own lizard brain. Part of this comes from a brain function known as mirroring. **We tend to reflect and respond in kind to people we are around**. That starts in infancy when Mommy smiles and baby smiles back. It continues in the sixth grade when Billy puts up his fists and Martin puts his up in response.

When we mirror behavior, we also set up cues to the brain for our chemistry to conform to our expression. Studies show that if we force a smile, our body responds with brain activity consistent with happiness. Other studies show that standing tall and acting confident increase our assertive behavior and cause others to respond to us as being in charge.

Remember how important "officer presence" is. You heard about it in the academy. The FBI studies on officer murders theorize that officer presence may be a factor in an offender's decision to kill, and a recent Force Science Institute study on car stops included officer demeanor as a risk factor in being attacked.

The bottom line is that, once again, you must be aware of your lizard F3 as soon as possible, engage your logic brain, and determine your own posture and demeanor by choice. *If you get sucked into mirroring the other person's aggression or succumb to the fight, flight, or freeze impulse, then you have less and less control over the outcome.*

Another self-control technique that helps control brain impulses is to reframe your situation. For example, as you ask an angry person what his name is, you approach that from a frame of "I'm gathering data on this person so that I can win most effectively. His response will be helpful to me winning," rather than "I'm going to see if this guy is going to respect me, and if he doesn't, I'm going to get my nightstick out and teach him some respect."

Self-talk is not just a motivational speaker's cheesy technique to build your self-esteem. It does, in fact, change brain chemistry and aligns behavior with high-level awareness and intentionality.

As you assess a person's ability to communicate logically, you can then continue to be aware of the F3 forces at work and help him bring his thinking from lizard autopilot to logic brain awareness. This will be an incremental process addressing the stressors cueing his F3 response that are within your control.

Did you catch that I said some of his stressors are within your control? The reason is that when you get to a scene, you ADD to the stress! This is the opposite of what we want to do, right? Didn't you tell your hiring board during your police interview that you wanted to be a law enforcement officer so that you could help people?

It doesn't take long for the reality of the hatred and anger that we encounter to live up to all of our officer survival indoctrination. After that, every encounter becomes about taking control. That's correct, by the way—we have to take control. But that can happen with our mental powers as well as with threats and force.

Another technique to mitigate the F3 response is to allow a person to save face. Remember that a threat to one's ego spikes the lizard brain's threat radar just like a physical threat can. As much as we always want to have the last word and make sure our subjects know we are in control, allowing a person some sense of victory will reduce their level of tension and resistance.

Hostage negotiators know this. It is especially important in surrender scenarios. "I won't come out unless I can bring my cat with me." Okay, bring your stupid cat. If that gives the subject a sense of having some control, his brain will see it as a win. The brain chemistry is the same whether winning by violence or winning by maintaining a defiant or controlling attitude—both have a calming effect.

## Chapter Eight

**The Broken Brain**

The principles of being aware of our own F3 impulses, how those impulses affect people we are dealing with, and how we can help move another person from lizard to logic brain are principles that apply to the average person.

Officers deal with average people a lot. But we also deal with more than our share of people who aren't average, and certainly with people who are not having an average day. *If they are in contact with a uniformed police officer, that automatically means it's probably not an average day!*

We talk about training police officers to "de-escalate." I dislike that term for a couple of reasons. One is that there is an implication that the initial "escalation" was the officer's fault in the first place. The other is that the term comes with an expectation that we can always "de-escalate" in an orderly and predictable way.

What this book advocates—based, of course, on brain science—is what I call "neural braking." I haven't talked about neural connections for the sake of simplicity, but they are a means for the areas of the brain to communicate. Our essential goal is to slow the rapid-fire panic connections made at the sub-awareness level by persons under stress (including the stress of police contact). We want to get them to move toward the logic brain and thiiiiiink.

Most communication courses operate from an underlying assumption that we're dealing with essentially rational people who can be "de-escalated," while a few are specifically focused on people with some type of impairment.

People with brain injuries, biochemical imbalances, physical impairments, and developmental disabilities will act, react, and respond differently than you or I would.

But people whose brains and bodies are functioning in a healthy way can still have moments—or stages of life—when they are not functioning at capacity. You and I will respond differently during times in our lives when we are experiencing grief, dealing with illness, or being otherwise adversely affected by stress in our lives.

And people who have had a lot of conflict or violence in their lives (including police officers) have a cumulative loss of control over their aggression responses. Some of these people are on the edge of losing control all of the time. They are dangerous. ***Excessive reactions to threats tend to snowball and feed off of themselves with no additional stimulus needed.*** Getting these types of people back to logic brain awareness is very difficult.

We play the odds that say that 70 percent of the people we interact with are normal, and they in turn respond pretty much as expected. And because they are the usual course of events, those normal responses become the beaten pathways through our own brains where we store the templates of our expectations in dealing with people.

We know that being a police officer changes the nature of our interactions with normal people, and that we are likely to be encountering people who are stressed out—either by whatever made them call the police in the first place or by our mere presence. **Dealing with upset, stressed-out normal people is our normal.** We tend to give people quite a bit of latitude for their stress, and we expand our definition of what constitutes normal behavior.

But sometimes that benefit of the doubt can be deadly. Remember our reference to dissonance? Something just doesn't feel right? Since we already know that our presence is a stressor to people, we may mentally calm our distress by telling ourselves, "They seem awfully nervous—but then, maybe I would too in their shoes." That's nice, but if you're getting that "vibe" that something isn't normal, it's time to thiiiiiink!

Nervous is normal, but skittish isn't. Bouncing on tiptoes isn't. Looking past you or over his own shoulder isn't. Tapping on his waistband isn't. Make sure you pay attention to the signs of tension that don't align with the normal nervousness of being stopped by a cop. Nervousness due to guilt is different and presents itself differently.

The other kind of "not quite right" response that should light up our awareness is the person who isn't normal. Consider the fact that 26 percent of Americans have a diagnosable mental illness, with half of those having more than one disorder. Although only 6 percent of the population has a serious mental illness, and most mental illnesses are not related to violence, *for those who do act out, police contact is highly likely.*

Nearly 10 percent of the population will have a mood disorder in any given year, and major depression affects nearly 7 percent in a given year. People affected in this way may have higher aggressiveness or lowered F3 responses. A muted F3 will result in the people we contact exhibiting less anxiety than we anticipate. A person who seems to have no fear of us is frightening to us.

An average of nearly four percent of the population will seriously contemplate suicide in any given year. Twenty percent of the nation is on psychiatric medication. Among college students, incoming freshmen are medicated at a rate of one in four for depression, ADHD, and a variety of other behavioral or mental health issues. Some of these medications can actually increase suicidal thoughts and behaviors. Mixed with alcohol, marijuana, or other drugs, the outcomes are unpredictable.

An estimated 30 percent of the population will have drug dependency problems at some point in their lives. The high level of paranoia and secrecy in the lives of addicts makes them dangerous because they are often in possession of illegal drugs and have a lot to lose. In addition, withdrawal can cause bizarre behavior.

Sixteen percent of the population has a hearing impairment. More than a million persons in the U.S. are legally blind. One in seven has a learning disability. Eighteen percent of all Americans are classified as having a disability.

One percent of the U.S. population has some level of autism, which is apparently increasing in frequency. Autism encompasses a range of behaviors, but can manifest itself in quick panic, an inability to make eye contact, a poor ability to communicate, hypersensitivity to touch or other stimuli, and other behaviors that would challenge an officer expecting normal responses.

Perhaps 1 in 25 people is diagnosable with psychopathy. This inability to process genuine emotion or have empathy for others often goes unnoticed. These folks can be dangerous because they don't have the same level of moral conscience as the rest of us. They are also very good at mimicking real emotion. Psychopaths are excellent observers and actors because, unlike most of us, they can see the world without emotional interference. They are very convincing.

Nine percent of the population has limited English proficiency. One quarter of the population has an IQ under 90 (90 is at the lower end of normal intelligence; the average IQ of police officers is 104). People with limited verbal skills are subject to more frustration. Similarly, mice are more aggressive than apes because apes have more ways of expressing themselves, expanding their options for dealing with others.

Given all of these variables, what are the odds that you are going to be dealing with a person who processes thoughts and information in the same way you do?

How frequently do you encounter a suspect, victim, or witness with no cognitive impairment, not under the influence of alcohol or other drugs, in complete control of their emotions and behavior, and who is not physiologically undergoing high stress?

If you find yourself living a day on patrol when everybody you contact is as together as you are, that might be the day to buy a lottery ticket. (And don't forget your own stress level, family and financial problems weighing on your mind, health issues, and fatigue!)

Our normal intervention techniques for normal people won't work the same way on any number of the impaired population. This is a critical piece of knowledge that must remain part of our basic operational awareness.

A person under the influence of alcohol is probably your most common interaction. There is no other drug more commonly associated with violence than alcohol! Half of all violent crimes and over 80 percent of murders are alcohol related.

Studies in mice show a 200 percent increase in aggressiveness under the influence of alcohol. While high doses of alcohol produce a sedative effect, lower levels are associated with aggression, risk taking, and self-defense aggression. The first part of the brain affected by alcohol is the logic brain. The filter that keeps us behaving seems to dissolve with liquor.

Just as we should "test" a person's F3 level by trying to determine if the individual has some logic brain functioning, we should also make quick assessments of his or her level of normality. Let me note here that I realize advocates for the disabled would object to my implication that a disabled person is abnormal. I only mean that, based on a graph of cognitive, emotional, and physical averages, some people are not in the middle of the bell curve.

If a person seems to be ignoring us, that's one of those ego offenses that really annoys most people, and even more so police officers. If you don't consider that the person might be hearing impaired or in shock, you may be setting up a tragic use of force incident that won't be forgiven.

A case in Colorado involved a cognitively disabled adult who did not have the physical appearance characteristic of some developmental disabilities. At a movie theater, the young man enjoyed the first showing of a movie so much that he wanted to stay for another show without a new ticket. The manager called police for what amounted to a theft of services call. Whether the disabled man didn't understand that he needed to purchase another ticket or was already in the process of arranging another purchase on his iPhone isn't entirely known.

When approached by police, the man, who was rather large, was not able to communicate and was averse to physical contact. He panicked and resisted, and was ultimately subdued by four police officers. The man died during the encounter after being restrained. A grand jury cleared the officers of wrongdoing.

I understand the uninformed civilian world making emotionally sympathetic decisions about police conduct based only on YouTube videos or news reports. People will side with the resister if the person shot or struck by police was young, old, having a birthday or about to get married, trying to turn his life around, or any of the other sob stories that you hear their mothers telling the reporters at the scene. It is frustrating, but understandable.

In the Colorado case, I don't want to second-guess the officers, and I don't expect any officer to have psychic powers. I had a similar experience recently with a pot-smoking autistic college student who was also on psychotropic medication that, when mixed with THC, caused him to lose bowel control. We both yelled a lot.

In reviewing a case like that of the man in the theater, we can learn a couple of things. One is my rule: If you have time to think, THIIIIINK! Sometimes redeployment is a more winnable strategy. We can what-if a situation to death. What if the person was a danger or had a weapon or was acting strangely because he was on unpredictable hallucinogenic drugs? If that were the case, a decision by the officers to break contact and ask management to call when they could contact him with a summons later could have had disastrous results.

But what if they had decided that fighting over an eight-dollar movie ticket wasn't worth handling the situation with that level of intensity? Were there alternatives? How far back in the contact could the first contact officer have assessed that the man was cognitively disabled and not able to respond to their requests and demands?

Every officer has an approach routine that works pretty well most of the time. It may be a standard, department-mandated contact routine or one that is part of your department culture. My question is do you have a backup plan? Does your current contact method incorporate an assessment of your contact's F3 logic capacity? Are you mentally thrown for a loop if you don't get the response you expect? If that's the case, then your lizard brain is going to perceive aberrations as a threat and throw some F3 on you that probably will not help you much in the situation.

Another abnormal kind of person that we encounter is the female offender. Again, by "abnormal" I simply mean not your average contact. The fact is most offenders are male, most drivers are male, and most police officers are male.

Women tend to self-select as aggressors when it comes to police interaction. By this I mean that women who are involved in crime, delinquency, and violence tend to have more violent tendencies as a group than men do. In other words, the line between non-criminal males and criminal males isn't that bright or broad, but the line between non-offending females and their criminal sisters is more distinct.

The significance of this is that, even though you are less likely to encounter a female offender compared with the probability of encountering a male offender, the female offenders you do encounter are more likely to be aggressive and assaultive than their male counterparts.

Another category of offender is the teenage offender. This group, too, is self-selecting in that we may find more violent tendencies in the subcategory of teen offenders. Of course, for those of you who work in high-density gang territory, youths may be conditioned and trained in violence and fear far beyond any normal developmental understanding of aggression and self-control.

Adolescents most actively develop templates for perception and response between the ages of 14 and 17. Despite what we might think, young people in this age category have good success in getting thought processes to their logic brain and deciding that submitting and cooperating with you makes the most sense. This is because, in most cases, they have not yet had enough perception/response experiences to have beaten down a neural pathway to an autopilot F3 response to you.

Nearly 20 percent of the population is made up of 17- to 24-year-old males. This demographic makes up a huge percentage of our arrests and contacts. Life experience at this age is limited, while testosterone seems unlimited! We should not underestimate the capacity for good citizenship in this age bracket, but we do know that pathways to the logic brain are still in development at this age.

## Chapter Nine

**How Your Smile Can Kill You**

FBI and Force Science findings suggest, and I agree, that a professional tone is the most effective and safest approach in any encounter. The overly friendly, good ol' boy interaction is an example of familiarity breeding contempt. Remember that posture and facial expression trigger a person's body chemistry to match the act. Your body chemistry and thinking actually become congruent with your posture or affect. (Affect—pronounced with a hard "a," as in "hatchet"—is the way in which one exhibits emotion.)

An overly friendly affect will necessarily reduce your alertness level. Your posture, language, and facial expression will cause your linking brain to suppress the tension that you should be feeling during a contact.

Using an overly friendly approach will also cause you to relax too soon, since you'll be primed to accept that everything is just fine. You may also experience a momentary mirroring effect with the person you are interacting with that will trick your brain into thinking that he is friendly too. This will reduce tension and also reduce your reaction time.

Another problem with the overly friendly approach is that when the subject's response isn't congruent—he doesn't mirror your niceness—it's hard to switch gears and become authoritative. The tendency is to stay friendly or even get friendlier, or try to continue to act friendly while your lizard brain is vying for your attention with some F3 chemistry. ***Your brain and body are literally getting mixed signals, and that will slow your reaction time.*** This actually causes more tension in the subject, because now his lizard brain is sensing the incongruence and is going into F3 mode. Altogether a bad combination.

The opposite of the overly friendly approach is the overly authoritative approach. The authoritarian approach relies on the subject feeling fear. We know that fear will push the subject's body chemistry toward fight, flight, or freeze, and the authoritarian is banking on some degree of freeze.

In a contact with a person of normal cognitive ability, most people will comply no matter what approach you use. As long as they are not overwhelmed with stress in addition to the stress of your presence, they will likely deal with the contact in a very normal way. They may be upset, they may be indignant, they may grin and bear it, but they are low-threat.

An overly authoritative approach is tension-inducing by design. Using this in a normal contact can unnecessarily ratchet up the subject's anxiety level and trigger resistance or flight. If we rely on some level of the freeze response—fear, interpreted by the authoritarian as respect—compliance may result. Submission in a confrontation is as much a survival instinct as is fighting to win. Remember, even in the animal kingdom, a decision to give up can mean that the subject lives and gets to walk away. In a sense, it is flight in the form of a slow retreat.

If a person is predisposed to hostility or is fearful about the contact because they are actually guilty of something, ***the overly authoritarian approach can trigger a full fight-or-flight resistance.*** Some officers know this very well and actually hope for this outcome and the attendant adrenaline rush. For me, as I tell my officers, I'm not too old to fight, but I'm too old to want to!

In an intense contact where you have a known suspect and the probability of a fight or chase is omnipresent, a very aggressive approach obviously makes sense and carries less risk than other approaches. You already have a suspect in fight-or-flight mode. The suspect will either have a lizard brain message that says that freezing or submitting is the best survival mode, or the logic brain will kick in and tell the suspect that giving up makes the most sense.

The transition from high stress to logic takes one main ingredient: time. It may be the time it takes for a suspect to get fatigued. Time may pass while a suspect is cornered or ordered to put his hands behind his back, and you can see in the delay that he's mentally exploring his options. Next to immediate compliance, this delay is the most useful thing for you. It tells you that he is either considering surrendering or moving back into fight-or-flight mode.

Even if he kicks back into fight-or-flight mode, it will now be a logic brain decision—he thinks that's the best choice for winning—and not a lizard brain decision. If that's the case, the intensity of his fight-or-flight chemistry will be somewhat diminished because of the conflict in his own brain about what course to take. You'll still have to subdue him, but it might be a little easier to do that than if he were fighting from a primitive place in his brain.

On the other hand, stress diminishes a person's capacity for decision making. In short, stress makes you stupid. If a suspect, like all the super-villains in the movies, is in cognitive mode with his stress under control while you are operating under your own fight-or-flight chemistry, he could be planning an effective strategy to deal with you.

The battle between these varying levels of response can be seen in officer contact videos. In some you see the officer trying to be friendly while the suspect is giving off all kinds of stress signals. In others you see the officer relying on the suspect's logic brain to kick in with repeated commands in deadly-force situations.

When a subject is not acting in the way that our behavior template has programmed us to expect, there is an error alert that hits our F3 button, and we re-evaluate and respond with a new strategy. However, the time it takes to turn that ship around may be too much to respond to a new and unexpected threat.

Repeated commands to a subject make a lot of sense from a brain science perspective, because stress changes and narrows perception. A suspect under stress may not see or hear you accurately enough to respond as quickly as you'd like. Think of your spouse trying to get your attention while you're paying attention to your inner thoughts (or the game on TV): "Honey . . . honey . . . HONEY . . ." until—"ROBERT!!"—it finally clicks.

If a deadly weapon is coming on target and the target is you, the person with the weapon forfeits any right to any verbal warning at all. Stop the threat right then. Don't rely on your ability to convince the other person to stop the threat!

The reason that I recommend a standard professional approach, with confidence and good posture, is that it makes sense from a brain perspective. First of all, your own affect (the way your body reflects your emotional state) will be congruent (lined up and making sense) with the body chemistry you need to deal with the contact.

Second, if the contact mirrors your behavior, he too will act professionally (rationally, attending to the reality of the situation).

Third, a professional approach does not project a personal hostility or threat to the subject. Therefore, the normal subject will not experience enough threat perception to kick his lizard brain into the fight-or-flight response just because you are stern, serious, or dispassionate.

I've seen officers have success with saying something like "It's just my job" in order to remove the sense that the encounter is a personal vendetta or affront to the suspect. The idea seems to convey a sense of commonality with the working man that most people who have had to do unpleasant things at their own job understand.

When a person senses a personal attack on their ego or identity, the lizard brain treats it like a physical threat, because **insults are often precursors to assaults**. If the person doesn't hand over some identification when you first ask, you'll get better results with "Sir, state law requires persons in the park after dark to provide identification. I'm sure you want both of us to act within the law" than with "Because I said so. Show me your ID now. I'm not asking you again." By the way, I'm not against the "or else" approach if being heavy-handed seems necessary. The problem with "or else" is that you have to be ready to administer the "else" and defend it later if things go badly. ***Never make threats. Only make promises you can keep.***

Fourth, the professional approach is neutral enough that it gives you the important ability and opportunity to assess the subject's reaction. If the subject is overly friendly, that's not congruent with the situation and you should sense a red flag. If the subject reacts in a highly defensive or aggressive manner, that's another red flag because you weren't presenting a threat in the way the overly aggressive approach would have.

Finally, the professional approach looks a lot better than any other approach on YouTube or when played for a jury or while being reviewed in an internal investigation.

Please remember that I'm not making these suggestions for the sake of public relations. They are designed to help you reduce anxiety in your subject in order to gain compliance and reduce the probability of having to fight. These suggestions also put you in a mental zone where you are able to more quickly and accurately assess danger signs so that you can react more quickly. It's not about being nice; it's about winning the encounter. It just happens to look nicer.

Another aspect of professionalism to keep in mind is during the handcuffing and physical custody stage. This is a critical stage of an arrest. It is the peak time for assaults on officers. A subject who is complying and not actively resisting has two advantages. The first is that he has controlled his F3 response and now is thinking and planning more clearly. He also has more dexterity and clearer sensory awareness than he would under high stress.

The second advantage is that his compliance has likely tuned down your own F3 chemistry. The timing of a cooperative arrest also may coincide with a recession of your adrenaline-induced strength. Your body is anxious to go into restoration mode after an F3 surge and may begin to relax prematurely.

Ideally, we don't want to be riding the same wave of adrenaline as our adversary if we have to engage in physically restraining a suspect. The most highly potent stage of F3 can be over in less than a minute. An all-out, life-or-death fight can lead to paralyzing exhaustion. Peak activity happens as early as 15 seconds, after which a significant decline often occurs.

This is why early recognition of dangerous aggression is key (as is being in good physical condition yourself). You want to enter the fight fast and win it fast. Blitz attacks on officers are, unfortunately, very effective. Even though you may be well trained in arrest control tactics, we are also conditioned to engage cognitively when we use force. The fact that we are reacting along with the fact that we may have to go through a mental evaluation process will slow us to a distinct disadvantage.

Even the way that many departments refer to fighting skills as "defensive" tactics keys a word into our decision-making process that may take a millisecond off of our response time when executing with speed is essential.

If we fail to gain control of a subject within 15 seconds, we may find ourselves in a declining F3 stage at the same time that the subject is peaking in his. This is why I am happy to see the disappearance of the use of force continuum as a training and policy doctrine. We cannot afford to allow a resisting subject to test our level of force through the failure of one technique after another until we get it just right.

Hopefully, as you are calculating some worst-case resistance scenarios, you have time to mentally choose your most appropriate weapon. Doing a mental inventory of your weapons systems will slow your response time. Making a transition from hands-only to pepper spray to baton is a time-consuming process, both in decision making and execution, especially considering the diminished fine motor skills resulting from your own F3 response.

Now is the time to appeal to the arrestee's logic brain. Using a professional and confident tone of voice for making commands and getting compliance at each step helps cement a "yes" mindset. It's an old sales technique. Next time you're working on buying a car or appliance, notice how often the salesperson gets you to agree on noncontroversial things. "You want a good value, right?" "If I could get you into this for less than fifty bucks a month could you afford that?"

Confusion is also a tension builder. Work with your fellow officers to have a good contact and cover routine. Having one officer yelling "Don't move!" while another is yelling "Hands up!" is going to generate some F3.

Even if the commands are consistent, if the suspect's brain is flooded with different voices from different directions, his compliance time will be slowed. When the goal is to slow a suspect's reaction time, sensory flooding can be helpful. But dogs barking, radios blaring, and multiple officers yelling will slow compliance. That may be okay, and it may be unavoidable, but even smart, self-aware criminals can't act outside of their biological limitations.

If you are dealing with a truly innocent person (or one who thinks he is), the slowness of compliance will probably be evident as he or she processes this traumatic encounter. An experienced officer can accurately discern genuine confusion from passive aggression (the guilty person who is stalling for time or trying to confuse the officer).

Giving incremental commands engages the suspect's cognitive process and gives him fewer resources to plot a defense or escape. Be careful that you don't keep talking all the time, because you don't have the capacity to talk and react at the same time. Make your narrative short so that if you need to react, you won't have to shift gears from your mouth to your hands.

Tension also occurs when a person doesn't know how an event is going to end. No television show goes to commercial without leaving you with a plot question that you have to stay tuned to get answered! Doctors and dentists these days are likely to tell you exactly what's going to happen in order to reduce your nervousness. "I'm going to put this bitewing in, and I'll need you to press down. It will feel a little uncomfortable but it won't be in there very long. Do you have any questions?"

The brain thrives on feedback. The linking brain and logic brain are scanning both input and memory to constantly assess threats and form various response strategies. If the body gets the message that a threat is diminishing, it can start calming down in as little as a few seconds.

If you have the time and the situation is stable enough, you can help engage the logic brain by giving step-by-step commands, repeating them, asking if the subject understood them, reminding them to do only what you say, nothing more or less, and monitoring compliance.

Consider, too, all of the noise in the subject's brain. With normal sensory perception we process literally millions of inputs per second. Skin cells gauge pressure, temperature, and pain; the ear maintains balance, interprets sounds, calculates distance, searches the memory for familiarity, and sends words to the brain to be defined and interpreted in the context of inflection, rate, volume, and texture; the eyes pull in light, reflection, colors, and shapes; even the nose can detect and interpret smells below our awareness level (that's another reason our confidence is important—people really can smell fear!).

Now add to that internal noise a couple of police officers screaming, radio static, tones and numbers blaring, police lights flashing. These are not stressors for us; they are comforts. That is the pond we swim in—radio chatter and flashing lights. We love it! But to the brain of the uninitiated suspect, it is noise and can create overload. Repeated, clear instructions (especially in the right ear of a right-handed person) can cut through the noise and be grabbed by the suspect's brain. Hearing goes to the brain faster than visual cues, which have to be processed through the retina first. When delivered simultaneously, visual cues given in addition to auditory cues will greatly enhance comprehension.

Most suspects are ordered to face away from arresting officers, so auditory cues (verbal commands) have to take precedence.

We might not want to go to that extent—some officers talk way too much—but giving the subject a sense of what's going to happen can help reduce the tension level:

"I appreciate your cooperation, Mr. Crook. I need to put these handcuffs on, and I know you don't want anyone to get hurt, so listen very carefully and do only what I tell you to do, or I'll have to assume you're trying to hurt me. Do you understand? When we get downtown I'll make sure you get treated right and can make a phone call, okay?"

You might also ask if he has been arrested before, and if he says that he has (or you know he has), ask how that went. If he was treated professionally, then reminding him that this arrest is no more threatening than the previous one may reduce his anxiety.

On the other hand, if he is resistant or panicked because the last time he was arrested he got injured, attacked at the jail, or wrongly treated in some other way, you might be able to reduce his fears and resistance by validating his concerns ("That must have been frustrating") and making assurances ("You know me, Red Dawg, I'll treat you fair"). Notice I'm not asking you to agree with his experiences or opinions, but just to agree that he felt a certain way. That's a noncommittal validation that can have a calming effect.

Once you get the compliant (but possibly plotting) person in a good position to handcuff, you might want to ask a question that he will verbally answer as you are moving in to apply the cuffs. Having him answer a question—even a yes or no question—will occupy enough of his brain that you should have him hooked up before he is able to shift his mental gears from thinking about your question to verbally responding to deciding that now is the time to fight you.

If he doesn't answer, his silence may indicate that his brain is engaged in planning an escape or an attack. Undistracted, he will have an accurate sense of your proximity to him from the sound of your movements, the shadows cast by your movements, and even your smell, as that sense is also enhanced under stress.

Getting both cuffs on in under half a second will dramatically lower the suspect's chances of moving, since it will take him only about a quarter of a second to sense that you are close enough for him to attack, resist, or escape. Obtaining a nod or a verbal response to a question, even if it elicits an unpleasant set of words, will provide you with the time advantage to act.

Remember that these verbal techniques work only when there is sufficient brain function in the suspect. If it is apparent that talking is accomplishing nothing, then the officer should effectively gain physical control rather than draw out a conversation that could prove counterproductive.

Suspects may use delay and conversation to plot an attack or escape, or to confuse you in ways that affect your own brain processes. If he is not at a physical or mental disadvantage, he is more likely to believe that he can launch a successful attack and escape—and he may be correct!

Officers are trained to give verbal commands in part for the sake of bystanders and video recordings. This practice has merit, but if you can articulate your observations and your need to force compliance, the phony words that take up valuable space in your head won't be necessary. Conversely, if you give a command and allow no time for compliance, your verbal intervention may seem like a pretext to a jury.

## Chapter Ten

**Let's Talk about You**

The policing profession has changed only incrementally with regard to the support available to its officers for brain health. Science has only recently begun unlocking our understanding of the biochemical and neurological bases underlying stress, memory, and even happiness.

If you are reading this because you are a police officer, let me say thank you. It's a crappy job in a lot of ways, even though so many of us, myself included, say that there is nothing like it and that we wouldn't want to do anything else. I left an academic's life working 35 hours a week, eight months out of the year, to return to the crazy shifts and crazy people in the police business.

Every job has its ups and down, plusses and minuses. I've been a truck driver, propane delivery driver, factory worker, preacher, insurance agent, farm worker, real estate appraiser, and soldier. As I write this, I am a lawman with decades of service, and I feel very blessed and privileged to serve in this way.

I also recognize that my career has been tempered by frequent respites as I've changed departments and even career paths from time to time. I haven't had to deal with the burnout of grinding along year after year with the same department. Just as with military service, I consider anyone who has spent even just a few years in law enforcement a veteran of police service, even if the relatively short term of service doesn't meet the profession's cultural definition of a "police veteran."

I have also been gifted with self-awareness as a result of my pastoral and chaplaincy experience, the research I have done in order to teach university classes in sociology, and the opportunities that training and writing have afforded me to meet hundreds of different law enforcement officers from sea to shining sea.

I will share with you that I have never considered suicide, but that I know perfectly healthy normal cops who have, and I have known cops who surprised me by killing themselves. I've had moments where my life was such that I could at least understand how a person could feel that suicide makes sense.

I have never been diagnosed with PTSD, but I have dealt with unidentified stress and anxiety that I traced to unresolved past events. One of my police heroes suffered and conquered PTSD with proper treatment.

I have never been divorced, but the "D" word has been spoken in my home. We're at 35 years now, so it looks like we're going to be okay. I understand how tough a police marriage can be.

Raised a teetotaling Baptist with an alcoholic grandfather as an argument for sobriety, I never succumbed to the temptation to cope with life by using alcohol, prescription drugs, or other substances. But I understand the tremendous influence of brain chemistry associated with substance abuse.

I have never had professional counseling. I was too proud and too suspicious to seek life coaching to accelerate problem solving in my life. I was often too proud even to turn to available mentors, preferring, like an adolescent, to do it myself. I say this not as a boast, but as a regret at my stubbornness and ignorance. Thankfully, good, wise friends have provided me with some of the best therapy for living life, and by the grace of God, I have survived emotionally.

In this final chapter, I simply want to increase your own self-awareness so that you can best maintain your brain health. We know that good nutrition and physical activity are necessary for physical health. And we know, mainly from advertisements, about heart health, dental health, bone health, sexual health, and more. But what do you know about your mental, spiritual, and emotional health? Let's just take a quick inventory:

Do you engage in intentional physical activity several times a week?

Do your meals have variety, including vegetables and protein?

Is your weight more than twenty pounds higher than it was ten years ago?

Do you have at least one activity that brings you pleasure unrelated to law enforcement?

Do you have a social group with whom you interact on a regular basis outside of law enforcement?

Do you read books unrelated to law enforcement?

Do you spend more than two hours every day playing video games, on the Internet, or watching television?

If you are in a family relationship, do you spend daily, intentional time with those significant persons in your household?

Do you have a budget that includes savings and reducing your debt?

Do you get six to ten hours of sleep during your sleep cycle on a regular basis?

Have you had a physical within the past two years?

Do you have a regular practice of prayer, meditation, or other quiet time?

Check your shoulder muscles right now—are they tight? Can you relax them if you concentrate on it?

Have I made you feel guilty or weird yet?

There's an old joke about a farmer who gets visited by a new college graduate with an agriculture degree who is working as a county agent. He offers the farmer some advice on how to improve operations, and the farmer says, "Son, I ain't farmin' half as good as I know how already."

I'm sure that's true of all of us when it comes to our health and well-being. All I can really ask is that you do what you already know is good for you!

One of the most remarkable scientific discoveries about the brain in recent years is its plasticity. The brain can change! Personalities can change! Senses can change! Reaction time can change! Life outlook can change! You can fight off aging, depression, and negative responses! Here are some things that we know are good for your brain.

Exercise that improves circulation and oxygenation of the blood to your brain will improve performance. I won't repeat what dozens of free Web sites can tell you, but using one of those sites can help you track your caloric expenditure.

I was inspired by a motivational speaker some years ago at the Missouri Narcotics Officer Association Conference who pointed out some simple math about weight loss. The magic number is 3,000. That's the number of calories in a pound of weight. Once you calculate your typical daily calorie use (do an Internet search for "basal metabolism rate" and calculate yours), then you can decide how much you need to increase your activity or reduce your caloric intake to lose weight. Of course, I'm just assuming that's your problem, as there aren't many "too skinny" cops out there (although that was my problem when I started!).

Achieving weight loss may be as simple as cutting out one donut or one soda a day, or pushing a third of your food to the side of your plate for leftovers. It could mean taking a walk or stepping up your workout or doing a half hour of foot patrol daily.

I found a book on getting in shape, and although I didn't follow every suggestion, my awareness level went up. I also use a free online fitness tracker. Between starting to feel frumpy, the shocking prospect of buying some new 46-inch-waist pants, and the decision to do some simple math and buy a fitness book, I lost 35 pounds and have managed to maintain a level of fitness that could easily have slipped away and plunged me into old age much faster than necessary!

Making sure you get plenty of non-caffeinated hydration is a universal and easily achievable health goal.

The easiest and quickest thing to do to improve your mental and physical health is stretching and breathing. Just a few minutes of intentional muscle use and slow breathing does wonders. Hold your breath for a bit after sucking in a good lungful from the diaphragm (using your shoulders to suck in the air is not as effective as using the muscle beneath your ribs), then hiss it out. Don't get dizzy, but do that a few times to flush out your system a bit.

A simple routine that you can do in your car or at your desk is a quick head to toe tense-and-relax session. Tense your toes, then your ankles, lower leg, thighs, buttocks, stomach, chest, fingers, arms, shoulders, neck, and even your face. Deliberately and with awareness, release the tension from your face, then your neck, and so on. It might help to imagine your tension melting into the floor and slowly breathing out as you do the relaxation.

One of the greatest benefits of this exercise for me is that it reminds me what tension feels like. I now often become aware of my shoulder muscles tensing—which seems to be the place my stress hits first—and then I can deliberately breath and relax.

Stress in your life is not a dysfunction any more than getting germs on your hands is unusual. The question is whether you give stress or germs the opportunity to defeat your natural defenses. Sometimes germs will get past your defenses and you will get sick. Likewise, sometimes stress will get the better of you. Both processes are well within the realm of normal, however, and also well within your control to manage under normal circumstances.

Another great thing for your brain is the positive influence of other people on your life. Being loved, engaging in conversation, laughing together, and crying together are all essential. Clubs, leagues, churches, and fraternal organizations are all brain-healthy (unless their activities revolve around vices).

Let's talk about your survival mindset. For years I've heard about the mythology of mindset. Positive thinking. The will to live. I've heard officers criticized for dying because they didn't have the will to live or the will to fight.

Frankly, as a rational person, it never made sense to me that we could somehow talk our bodies out of dying from a bullet wound. I'm a religious person, and the idea of mind over matter sounded more like religion than science.

Turns out, I was wrong. Because the brain is well connected to the rest of the body, our bodies not only respond to the brain (a stern frown appears when we think something is wrong), but our brain also responds to the body! For example, research shows more positive reactions when test subjects are asked to hold a pencil clenched in their teeth. This action forces the mouth and face muscles into an artificial smile. The brain says "Hey, the face is smiling, guess we'd better shoot some happy chemicals into the system!" And it does.

Another thing I was skeptical about was an assumption, drawn from FBI studies on law enforcement officers killed, that the officers' demeanor and appearance contributed in some way to their deaths. There were several reasons why this assumption seemed suspect to me as a researcher. The first was that the characteristics of the murdered officers were not measured in relation to surviving officers—in other words, there was no study of living officers' psychological and behavioral profiles to show that the murdered officers were any different.

Secondly, although still too frequent, the murder of police officers is statistically rare enough that there are few discernable patterns; they appear instead to be very random and unpredictable events. And finally, some of the anecdotal evidence came from interviews with cop killers years after their cases were finished. For some odd reason, I distrust statements about cops from murderers who say they felt like an officer's appearance and demeanor somehow gave them the idea that they could get away with killing them.

But I now know a few more things about humans. One study on car stops, done by the Force Science Institute, yielded an interesting observation by the person role playing as the driver in studies of approaches by officers to vehicles and their reaction times to assaults. The role player repeatedly sensed which officers would be vulnerable to attack.

The results of this study came to my attention at about the same time that I was reading studies on confidence and aggression. People going into a job interview thinking about a recent success were more successful in their interviews. Persons with a confident posture showed more positive outcomes with others. People with an overall life outlook of having control from within, rather than of being controlled by outside circumstances, have better outcomes by several measures.

In other words, brain science tells us that attitude changes outcomes! If the survival mindset is deep enough that it changes one's behavior, then it can also affect life and death. But a casual belief that the badge brings magical qualities to one's character may do more harm than good as a false pretense.

These intangible thoughts that translate into reality point to another amazing characteristic of our brain: the lizard brain and the linking brain are so in tune with sensory input that reality itself is relative.

A great friend of mine and legendary police officer-turned-psychologist-turned-priest once told me of one of his first professional counseling clients. The client was a woman who lived in an idyllic, isolated mountain home. She was a homemaker while her husband was away. In the course of her daily activities, she watched soap operas, listened to country music, and followed the police scanner. She came to my friend complaining of depression!

Nothing on the scanner or the daytime dramas or the plaintive country songs was actually happening to her, but her brain still responded with the chemistry designed to help her deal with those things as reality. A constant drain on stress chemistry can lead to fatigue and depression. The doc's prescription was pretty obvious.

Cops' brains are constantly bombarded by the lizard brain's panic messages. Our level of alertness—not just watching, but the actual brain chemistry of alertness—is fatiguing. Let's contrast two types of first responders: firefighters and cops.

Firefighters work and train as a team. They spend time together in the firehouse watching training films, eating together, and doing maintenance work that has a beginning and end with a visible result. When they get a fire call, their adrenaline peaks, they spring into action, and they go fight a fire or conduct a rescue. People love them and wave enthusiastically with all five fingers as they pass by. After the mission they return to the station, clean their equipment, and talk about the call.

This is a classic example of the kind of stress the body was designed for. There is social support, work with a visible reward, adrenaline spikes where the adrenaline gets burned up fighting a fire or coming back to the station to lift weights. After a fire call there is a natural decompression by doing maintenance work and chatting with colleagues.

Now let's look at the poor police officer. Out there alone, she listens to the police radio, getting vicarious adrenaline jolts from calls that aren't even in her jurisdiction. (The lizard brain cares nothing about reality. Whether it's a movie, a story, or an actual event, the lizard brain gets excited!) She gets many calls, but few of them require much physical effort, and without that there is no mechanism for burning off the F3 chemistry.

She has little interaction with other officers, and may even work under policies that forbid taking breaks with her colleagues. Her interactions with citizens are overwhelmingly negative and stress-filled. The friendly wave or getting her coffee paid for anonymously by an appreciative citizen is a rare treat and only punctuates how infrequently that occurs.

As she cruises her patrol area, her senses are constantly alive and cautionary. Every block reminds her of a crisis she has dealt with, every car is a potentially stolen vehicle, every person a potential suspect. She seldom debriefs at the station and has little time to calm down before she walks into her house after her shift only to be confronted with a needy family and plenty of things to do around the house.

Add to that some shift work, office politics, financial pressures, and you have a good recipe for pressure-cooked cop.

In addition to this cumulative stress where the F3 chemistry varies from a constant drip to a geyser, with the chemical antidote tank typically drained to empty, there are those individual events that can tax a human to capacity.

The injury or death of a partner or peer; the near-death encounters of crashes, shootouts, and fights; and career-threatening events all can create such a huge and sudden strain on the mind, body, and soul that some systems simply collapse.

Just as the brain can command the body to go into fight, flight, or freeze mode, so too the brain itself can withdraw into one of these states. In the short term, aggression, withdrawal, or numbness can give the brain time to heal. The problem occurs when these strategies stretch out over time and become stressors in themselves.

As I've repeatedly said, the most essential function of the brain is short-term survival. PTSD and related symptoms are short-term survival gone rogue.

If you have sleep disturbances, stomach and digestive problems, frequent illness, withdrawal from family and friends, lowered sex drive, frequent anger, constant low levels of feeling stressed, sudden attacks of panic and anxiety, overreactions to things that you used to handle calmly, more use of force, increased drinking or reliance on prescription drugs, or any general life changes that you or an objective person recognize as unhealthy, you may be under the influence of your survival brain stuck in an unhealthy response mode. An evaluation by a competent professional familiar with trauma would be a lifesaving investment.

# Afterword

I'm not getting any younger, and police work is no country for old men. With due regard for my fitness and competence, I've reached a point where no compliment comes without the appendage "for your age." I'm in good shape—for my age. I can really handle those midnight shifts—for a guy my age. I'm "still" a pretty good shot (amazing!) for my age.

There are lots of young stallions who still, despite all of my urgings to find another profession, want adventure, want to help people, want to live as constant and professional heroes.

To them I give the streets and bailiwicks and woods and rivers and trains and campuses and all manner of gatherings where humans do their business among predators. I hope that while I still live, and even beyond those days, this book and my travels will provide even a millisecond of advantage to the good guys.

Officers, I have always been proud of my calling. My badge has always represented many of the things I value most highly. I have survived, at least as I type these words, without the wounds that many of my friends, colleagues, and trainees have suffered in their service. Take your job seriously. Not just the task, but the calling. And by the way, thank you for your service. ***Stay safe!***

Thanks for spending time with me by reading *The Badge and the Brain*. If you'd like to visit with me some more, there are plenty of ways to do that, and I would appreciate hearing from you.

- Email me at jshults@joelshults.com
- Follow me on Twitter @ChiefShults
- Visit the Web site for Street Smart Force and Shults Consulting at JoelShults.com
- Visit the National Center for Police Advocacy at PoliceOfficersVoice.com
- Follow my blog, "The Police Perspective," at joeshults.blogspot.com

\*\*\*

*"May the grace of the Lord Jesus Christ, and the love of God, and the fellowship of the Holy Spirit be with you all"* – *2nd Corinthians 13:14 (NIV)*

## Suggested Reading

*The Biology of Violence*, Debra Neihoff

*Blink*, Malcom Gladwell

*Brain-Based Learning*, Eric Jensen

*Brain Bugs*, Dean Buonomano

*Brain Rules*, John Medina

*The Brain that Changes Itself*, Norman Doidge

*Change Your Brain, Change Your Life*, Daniel Amen

*Drive*, Daniel Pink

*The Emotional Life of Your Brain*, Richard Davidson

*The Gift of Fear*, Gavin DeBecker

*Healing the Angry Brain*, Ronald Potter-Efron

*How We Decide*, Jonah Lehrer

*Human Facial Expressions: An Evolutionary View*, Alan J. Fridlund

*Incognito*: Secret Lives of the Brain, David Eagleman

*The Invisible Gorilla*, Christopher Chabis

*Learning and Cognition*, Thomas Leahey

*Left of Bang*, by Patrick Van Horne

*Mental Endurance*, Chris McNab

*On Killing*, Dave Grossman

*The Owner's Manual for the Brain*, Pierce Howard

*The Political Brain*, Drew Westen

*The Power of Habit*, Charles Duhigg

*The Role of the Amygdala in Fear and Anxiety*, Michael Davis

*Spark*, John J. Ratey

*The Spiritual Brain*, Mario Beauregard

*Subliminal*, Leonard Mlodinow

*Teaching Smarter with the Brain in Focus*, Sarah Armstrong

*Thinking Fast and Slow*, Daniel Kahneman

*Tipping Point*, Malcom Gladwell

*Train Your Mind, Change Your Brain*, Sharon Begley

*A User's Guide to the Brain*, John Ratey

*Why Zebras Don't Get Ulcers*, Robert M. Sapolsky

*Your Brain at Work*, David Rock

*Your Survival Instinct Is Killing You*, Marc Schoen

The Badge and the Brain: Street Smart Force

Made in the USA
Charleston, SC
14 March 2015